PRACTICE BOOK

Reading, Writing, Grammar, Usage, and Mechanics

Unit **4** **Hit Series**

Unit **5** **Time Detectives**

Unit **6** **Community Quilt**

Cover: Club de Madres Virgen del Carmen of Lima, Peru

Copyright © 2000 by Scholastic Inc. All rights reserved.   Published by Scholastic Inc.   Printed in the U.S.A.

ISBN 0-439-09117-9

SCHOLASTIC, SCHOLASTIC LITERACY PLACE, and associated logos and designs are trademarks and/or registered trademarks of Scholastic Inc.

4 5 6 7 8 9 10   40   07 06 05 04 03 02 01 00

CONTENTS

UNIT 4 HIT SERIES

CONTENTS

UNIT 5 — TIME DETECTIVES

CONTENTS

UNIT 6 · COMMUNITY QUILT

★ NEWSLETTER ★

Welcome to *Hit Series*

Over the next few weeks, you'll be spending time with some very popular characters from TV, movies, and books. What makes these stories and shows so popular? That's for you to decide. Where did the ideas for these hit series come from? That's for you to find out! Sit back and relax. Your Anthology is about to take you on a tour of some all-time favorites.

What a Character!

Ms. Frizzle is at it again! You'll read a script from the Magic School Bus TV show. Then when you read a selection from *The Baby-sitters Club,* you'll understand how challenging a baby-sitting job can be.

 Check out a hundred-year time line of hits.

A SERIES FOR EVERYONE

You're bound to find at least one of your favorite series as you continue reading! You'll be figuring out *I Spy* riddles and joining Encyclopedia Brown as he tackles a case.

 **You'll also be chuckling over elephant jokes.**

Let's Visit a Publishing Company

Where do you go with your best-selling book idea? Take it to a publishing company! That's the place that turns a writer's words and ideas into a book. See what publishers do when they have a hit series on their hands.

★ NEWSLETTER ★

Let's Meet Joanna Cole and Bruce Degen

Cole is a terrific writer. Degen's drawings are just great. Together they have created two of the most popular book characters of the 1990s — Ms. Frizzle and her Magic School Bus. Discover just how they do it.

Long-Running Hits

Read a folk tale from the Southwest called *The Three Little Javelinas*. You'll soon see why the tale sounds so familiar. Then you'll read about one of America's most popular families and their many adventures in *Little House on the Prairie*.

+PLUS+ A colorful travel diary takes you to one of the places where the Ingalls lived.

Things You'll Do

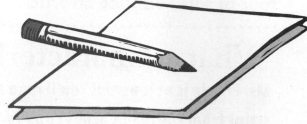

Everyone's a critic! Now you can be one, too. You'll be writing your own **series review**.

Who's your favorite book character? Are there too many to choose from? Soon you'll have to decide as you write a **character fact file**.

Here's your chance to take your favorite series and create a **new episode**. Maybe you'll even make a guest appearance!

Getting Started

Take a poll of five adults. Ask them what their favorite books were when they were kids. Bring these titles to school. Can you find any of them in your Anthology or library?

ADULTS

FAVORITE BOOKS

WELCOME TO THE PUBLISHING COMPANY

1. How do you think books are made?

   Students may think a person writes a story down and draws

   pictures, and then gives it to a company that copies it many times.

2. What do you think are the roles of the following people in creating a book: editor, designer, artist?

   Students may not know the names of different jobs. They may

   suggest that artists make the pictures.

3. What do you want to know about how to publish a book?

   Students may want to know about binding books or about

   how someone's story is chosen to be made into a book.

4. How do you think you could find out more?

   Students may suggest writing to publishing companies for information,

   looking in the library or encyclopedias for information, or visiting a

   publishing company.

STUDENT LOG

Here's a way to keep track of what you do in the Publishing Company.

Fill in the chart when you visit the Publishing Company.

Date	What I Did	What I Learned

A WALK IN THE DESERT

Draw a line from each word on the left to its definition on the right. Then label the drawings.

1. tumbleweeds

a. a hot, dry, sandy land with few or no plants or animals

2. desert

b. bushy plants that grow in the desert and are blown about by the wind

3. javelina

c. a wild pig that lives in the southwestern United States and in Mexico

4. adobe

d. a sandy kind of clay used to make bricks

5. coyote

e. a desert plant that has a thick stem covered with sharp spines instead of leaves

6. cactus

f. an animal that looks like a small, thin wolf

adobe   *coyote*   *tumbleweed*

Is it possible for a cactus to grow in your neighborhood? Explain your answer.

WORDS WITH *oi, oy*

The /oi/ sound can be spelled *oi* or *oy*. Read each clue in the puzzle. Then write the vowels that make the /oi/ sound.

1. What you speak with   v _o_ _i_ c e

2. What plants grow in   s _o_ _i_ l

3. What a male child is called   b _o_ _y_

4. What happy people feel   j _o_ _y_

5. What's at the end of a sharp pencil   p _o_ _i_ n t

6. What a decision is   c h _o_ _i_ c e

7. What nickels, dimes, and quarters are   c _o_ _i_ n s

8. What loud trains and planes make   n _o_ _i_ s e

9. What water does when it gets very, very hot   b _o_ _i_ l

10. What fruit will do if you leave it out too long   s p _o_ _i_ l

Which two words are highlighted?

_____coyote_____   _____coil_____

Write a paragraph using as many *oi, oy* words as you can.

CHARACTER TRAITS

Think about the characters in *The Three Little Javelinas*. What are they like? How do you know? Complete the chart below. Under Example, enter an example from the story. Under Character Trait, name the character trait the example shows.

	Example	Character Trait
Description	Coyote, who was very sneaky, tiptoed along behind.	sneaky
Actions	*The first little javelina wandered lazily along.*	*lazy*
Thoughts	*"Mmm! A tender juicy piggy," he thought.*	*greedy*
Words	*He called out sweetly, "Little pig, little pig, let me come in."*	*clever*

FOLK TALE SETTING

Retell a scene from the "Three Little Pigs" folk tale in a new setting. Use the boxes below to plan the scene.

Students' responses will vary.

MY NEW CHARACTERS:

MY NEW SETTING:

SCENE EVENTS:

Will my scene events be like those in the original story?

Have I chosen a new setting for my scene?

Will I use lots of details in describing the setting?

WRITER'S CHECK

COYOTE COMPLAINT

The three little javelinas have to fill out a police report on what happened to them. They have already answered one question. Help them answer the rest.

 **POLICE DEPT**

1. Officer: Against whom are you filing this report?

   Three javelinas: _____ We are bringing a complaint against the coyote. _____

2. Officer: What did the suspect do to you?

   First javelina: _____ He blew away my tumbleweed house. _____

   _____

   Second javelina: _____ He blew down my saguaro rib house. _____

   _____

   Third javelina: _____ He tried to blow down my adobe brick house, ____

   but he couldn't. Then he tried to slide down my stove pipe. ____

3. Officer: What did you do to the suspect?

   Third javelina: _____ I lit a fire inside my wood stove. _____

4. Officer: What happened to the suspect?

   Three javelinas: _____ He turned into a puff of smoke and ran away! ____

   _____

POSSESSIVE PRONOUNS

Read the sentences carefully. Underline each possessive pronoun and write to whom it refers on the line.

A possessive pronoun shows ownership.

Possessive Pronouns
my   your   his   her   its   our   their

1. Smithy called to Sarah and Willie. He said, "My toy dog is trapped." _____ *Smithy*

2. "His leg is caught." _____ *the dog*

3. The children put their heads together. _____ *the children*

4. "We'll save your dog," they said. _____ *Smithy*

5. Sarah rolled up her sleeves and pushed. _____ *Sarah*

6. Willie wrapped his arms around the toy dog's neck and pulled. _____ *Willie*

7. Soon, Smithy had his dog back. _____ *Smithy*

8. Its leg was a little torn, but that was all. _____ *the dog*

9. Sarah clapped her hands. _____ *Sarah*

10. She was happy she could free its leg. _____ *the dog*

Write three sentences about someone you helped. Use possessive pronouns in the sentences.

Name

DRAW YOUR OWN CONCLUSIONS

The sentences below come from *The Three Little Javelinas*. Circle a conclusion that can be made from each sentence. Write your own conclusion for the last sentence.

When you draw conclusions, look for details and ideas in the story. Put them together to form a new idea.

1. In this hot, dry land, the sky was almost always blue.
   a. This story takes place in a cold place.
   b. This story takes place in a desert.
   c. It rains almost all the time here.

2. The third little javelina thought a moment and said, "May I please have a few adobes to build a house?"
   a. The third javelina wants to build a strong, solid house.
   b. The third javelina cannot build a house.
   c. The third javelina wants to make adobes.

3. Coyote pretended to be very old and weak, with no teeth and a sore paw.

   Conclusion: _Possible answer: Coyote wants the javelinas to think that he is too weak to hurt them._

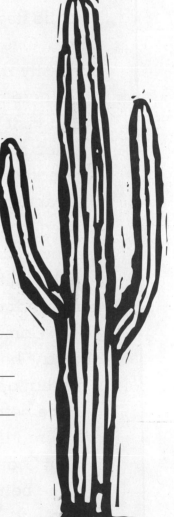

Describe the way the third javelina saved her brothers.

LITTLE RED

by Diane Galen-Harris

Read the story. Use it to complete page 17.

Once upon a time, there was a little girl who lived near the ocean. Her favorite color was red. Her boat was red. Her oars were red. Even her raincoat was red. People called her Little Red.

Little Red's grandma lived all alone on a nearby island. One day, Little Red was rowing her boat. Suddenly, a shark swam up behind her.

"Where are you going?" asked the shark.

"To visit my grandma," replied Little Red.

Then the shark swam to the island and yelled, "Grandma!"

Grandma thought it was Little Red calling, so she walked to the shore. Then she saw the shark. She ran away, dropping her cap. The shark put it on.

When Little Red got to the island and called for her grandma, the shark answered, "I'm having a swim. Come join me." Little Red looked around and saw her grandma's cap bobbing in the water.

"What a big nose you have," she said.

"The better to smell your flowers with," answered the shark.

"But Grandma, what big teeth you have," she said.

"The better to eat you up!" cried the shark, who jumped at Little Red. But Little Red's grandma had returned. "Take that, you old shark!" she said as she hit him. He swam off, never to return.

My questions and ideas as I read

Encourage students to use this space to record their questions and ideas as they read.

Copyright © Scholastic Inc.

DRAW CONCLUSIONS

Look at the story "Little Red." Complete the chart. Tell what conclusions you can draw about each of the characters. Then give your reasons for each conclusion.

When you draw conclusions, you use information from the story and what you already know to make judgments.

MY CONCLUSIONS   MY REASON

MY CONCLUSIONS	MY REASON
About Little Red: *Possible answer: Little Red is smart and adventurous.*	*Goes to see her grandma by herself; doesn't believe the shark.*
About the shark: *Possible answer: The shark is hungry and clever and wants to eat Little Red.*	*In the original story, the wolf wants to eat Little Red Riding Hood. I think the shark is a lot like this wolf.*
About Grandma: *Possible answer: Grandma is brave.*	*She comes back to face the shark and save Little Red.*

Write another ending to "Little Red."

STORY SETTING

Look back at the story to find each sentence shown in the chart. Then find and write the picture details the artist used to show the scene.

Story Sentences	Picture Details
p. 14: Steep purple mountains looked down on the desert, where the cactus forests grew.	*steep purple mountains, cactus plants, dry desert*
p. 17: The second little javelina walked for miles among cactus plants called saguaros.	*hot desert sun, saguaro plants, rattlesnake, dry bones*
p. 20: So the third javelina built herself a solid little adobe house cool in summer and warm in winter.	*adobe house*
p. 25: And if you ever hear Coyote's voice way out in the desert at night . . . well, you know what he's remembering.	*Coyote sitting atop rocks, howling at the moon at night. Desert cacti and other plants.*

Suppose the illustrator decided to illustrate the first three sentences on page 20. What might he have drawn?

ILLUSTRATOR'S CRAFT

Suppose that *The Three Little Javelinas* took place in an entirely different setting, such as a rain forest or a modern city. How would the illustrator dress the javelinas? What picture details would show the setting? Jot down a few ideas. Then draw a picture of the three javelinas in the new setting.

My ideas: _____ *Answers will vary.*

_____

_____

_____

DIPHTHONG /oi/ *oi, oy*

All the scrambled words have *oi* or *oy* in them. Unscramble the letters to make a word that completes the sentence. Write the word in the sentence. The first one has been done for you.

1. We took a bag of _____coins_____ to the bank. (n s o i c)

2. The woman said, "Please _____join_____ us for dinner." (o j i n)

3. You can wrap the food in _____foil_____ and put it away. (l o f i)

4. Roy _____pointed_____ his finger and said, "I want that toy." (t o p i e n d)

5. The cook will bake or _____broil_____ the fish. (l i b o r)

6. The _____voice_____ on the phone was loud and clear. (i e c v o)

7. There were nine _____boys_____ on each team. (y o b s)

8. Too much rain might _____destroy_____ the crops growing in the fields. (y e t o d s r)

9. A loud _____noise_____ woke up the baby. (s e i o n)

10. Some students will _____enjoy_____ reading the book about sharks. (j n e y o)

Work with a partner to write riddles about words with *oi* and *oy*. Give your riddles to a classmate to solve.

TEST-TAKING: NONFICTION

Read the passage. Then follow the directions and mark your answer choices.

Native Americans of the Southwest

Long ago, Native Americans settled in the Southwest. The desert area was hot and dry. There was very little rainfall. So the Desert People tried to build their houses near a river or stream.

The Native Americans mixed clay, stones, and grass to make adobe bricks. This was the building material of their four- or five-story adobe homes.

Directions: Fill in the letter next to the words that best answer the question.

1. What are adobe bricks made from?

    (a) clay and rain

    (b) ashes

    (c) sticks and stones

    (d) clay, stones, grass

Directions: Fill in the letter next to the answer that best completes the sentence.

2. The purpose of the passage is to _____*inform*_____ .

    (a) persuade

    (b) inform

    (c) entertain

    (d) question

RIVER CROSSING

Read the definition of each word. Then use the words from the box to fill in the paragraph.

canvas: a heavy, coarse cloth used for making tents, sails, and wagon covers

ford: a shallow part of a body of water that can be crossed by wading

splash: to hit or move through water so that it is thrown about

hitched: tied or fastened with a rope

lurched: having suddenly swayed in one direction or from side to side

running gear: the part of a wagon that the wheels and steering bar are connected to

The rider (1) _____*hitched*_____ the horse to the wagon with a rope.

Next he pulled the (2) _____*canvas*_____ cover over the wagon. Then

he bent down to make sure that the (3) _____*running gear*_____ was secure

and the wagon was safe for steering. He guided the horse into the

(4) _____*ford*_____ , where the river could be crossed. Suddenly, a

tree branch fell into the water with a (5) _____*splash*_____ . The horse

(6) _____*lurched*_____ , or swayed, in the other direction. Finally, they

made it safely to the other side.

Write a scene for a western movie. Use at least two words from the box.

r-Controlled Vowel /ûr/ ur, ir, er

Read each group of words. Circle the word that has the vowel sound you hear in the word *her.* Then find a word from the box that rhymes with the one you circled. Write it on the line.

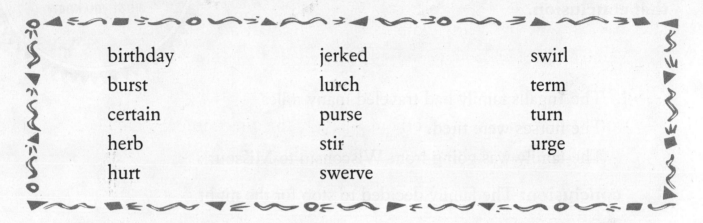

birthday	jerked	swirl
burst	lurch	term
certain	purse	turn
herb	stir	urge
hurt	swerve	

1. gem   great   (germ)   green   _term_
2. nice   (nurse)   near   north   _purse_
3. market   month   morning   (merge)   _urge_
4. (fur)   from   four   flare   _stir_
5. trust   (thirst)   tear   trip   _burst_
6. (whirl)   wear   weak   while   _swirl_
7. crisp   cork   (curb)   cream   _herb_
8. stair   (skirt)   score   spring   _hurt_
9. pear   press   pour   (perked)   _jerked_
10. crib   (church)   chair   crab   _lurch_

Choose one pair of rhyming words and write a rhyme. For example, *the nurse forgot her purse.*

DRAW CONCLUSIONS

Read each group of sentences from *Little House on the Prairie*. Then read the conclusion. Draw a line through any sentence that does not go with that conclusion.

Think clearly before you draw a conclusion. Combine story facts with what you know.

1. The Ingalls family had traveled many miles.
   The horses were tired.
   ~~The family was going from Wisconsin to Missouri.~~

   conclusion: The family decided to stop for the night.

2. ~~Mary and Laura were under the blanket.~~
   The wagon was swaying and turning.
   You could only see Pet and Patty's head in the water.

   conclusion: Pa knew the horses might not make it across the creek without his help.

3. ~~The sound of the water filled the air.~~
   Pa made sure the cover was tied tightly to the wagon.
   "The creek water is pretty high," Pa said.

   conclusion: Pa wanted the things inside the wagon to stay dry when they crossed the creek.

The Ingalls family is moving because the place where they lived had gotten too crowded. Write a sentence describing the kind of place you think they would like to live in now.

PREWRITING ORGANIZER

Travel Guide Entry: Preparing for a Trip

You will write a travel guide entry about preparing for a trip. Pack the suitcases below with notes as you plan and get ready to write.

Students' responses will vary.

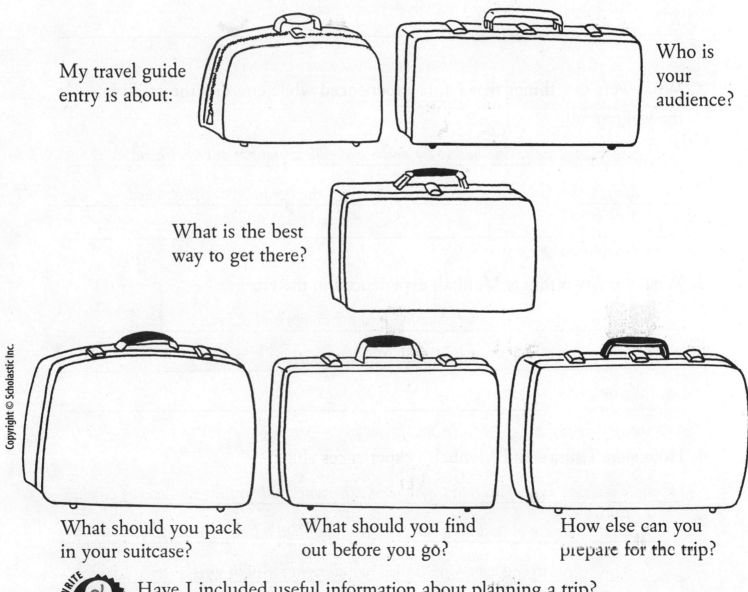

My travel guide entry is about:

Who is your audience?

What is the best way to get there?

What should you pack in your suitcase?

What should you find out before you go?

How else can you prepare for the trip?

Have I included useful information about planning a trip?

Will the reader learn something about traveling to a new place?

EXCITING TRIPS

1. Why do you think Laura Ingalls Wilder wrote about pioneer life?

Possible answers: She wanted to share her

childhood memories. She wanted others to learn

about what life was like in the 1800s and what the natural environment was like.

2. What were two things that Laura experienced while crossing the creek in the wagon?

Possible answers: She had to lie down and pull a blanket over her head.

She saw her father in the rushing water, and she became very frightened.

3. What were two things Meribah experienced in the creek?

Possible answer: She fell into the creek, and a leech

attached itself to her foot.

4. How were Laura's and Meribah's experiences alike?

Possible answer: Both girls had frightening experiences when they crossed the creek;

Laura's family almost drowned, and Meribah had a leech on her foot.

However, everything turned out all right for both girls.

COMPOUND SUBJECT AND PREDICATE

> A compound subject tells about two or more people, places, or things. A compound predicate has two or more verbs telling what the subject is or does.

Read the sentences. Underline each compound subject and circle each compound predicate.

1. <u>Ma, Pa, Laura, and Mary</u> leave the Big Woods.

2. <u>Pet and Patty</u> pull the covered wagon.

3. Jack (barks and trots) next to the horses.

4. <u>The grass and tree branches</u> blow in the wind.

5. The road (divides and turns) sharply toward the creek.

6. <u>Pet and Patty</u> (drink) from the creek (and graze) on the grass.

7. Pa (climbs) down from his seat (and ties) the wagon cover.

8. The wagon (lurches) forward (and sways) to the side.

9. <u>Laura and Mary</u> (grab) a blanket (and cover) their heads.

10. <u>Ma and Pa</u> (unpack) the wagon (and unhitch) the horses.

Write two sentences describing life on the prairie. Use compound subjects and predicates.

TOO CLOSE FOR COMFORT

Answer these questions about the order in which things happened in *Little House on the Prairie*. Page numbers from the story and signal time words are given to help you.

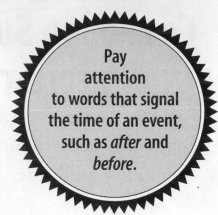

Pay attention to words that signal the time of an event, such as *after* and *before*.

Page 32. What happened *after* Pa turned south and went down the road?

Possible answers: The road went up and down. Then Laura gasped and clutched the wagon bow, because it looked as if there was no more land.

Pages 36–37. Pa tied down the wagon cover. What did he do *before* he unrolled the canvas? *He climbed down from the seat.*

Page 38. What did Ma say to the girls *after* the noise stopped?

She told them to lie down.

Page 40. What was Pa doing *before* Ma told Laura to lie down?

He was talking to the horses.

Page 41. *After* they got to the top of the bank, where did the wagon stand?

It stood safely out of the river.

THINK & WRITE Write about what would have happened if Pa had turned toward the west instead of the south. Be sure to use words that signal time.

BACK TO SCHOOL

by James Washington

Read the story. Use it to complete page 30.

At last, the harvest is in! Now I can go to school again. Before I leave for school, I put some bread, cheese, and apples in my sack for lunch. Next, I tie together a few pieces of wood to bring with me. The wood will be used to heat the schoolroom. My little brother and I leave early. It's a long walk to school.

We walk up a windy road. Later, friends join us along the way. We girls walk together in a group, and the boys run ahead.

When we get to school, the teacher, Miss Bloom, is at the front door. She is wearing a full long dress and high-button shoes. Then, inside the classroom, we pile up the wood. Miss Bloom has already made a fire in the wood stove, so the room is warm.

Next, we all go to our places. Children of all ages learn together in one room. The little ones sit in the front, while the oldest ones sit in the back.

Miss Bloom starts teaching us about words and numbers. Then we talk about faraway places we have never seen. Soon it is time to go home.

I love every minute of the day. How I've missed school!

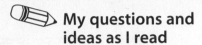 **My questions and ideas as I read**

Encourage students to use this space to record their questions and ideas as they read.

SEQUENCE

Fill in the chart. Read these sentences from "Back to School." Then write what happens next. Include the words that tell you the order in which things happen.

> Pay attention to words that show time, such as *first, then,* and *next*. These words can help you keep track of the order in which things happen in a story.

1. I put some bread, cheese, and apples in my sack for lunch.

Next, I tie together a few pieces of wood to bring with me.

2. My little brother and I leave early.

Possible answer: Later, friends join us along the way.

3. When we get to school, the teacher, Miss Bloom, is at the door.

Possible answer: Next, we all go to our places.

4. Miss Bloom starts teaching us about words and numbers.

Then we talk about faraway places we have never seen.

Suppose the girl in "Back to School" dropped her brother off at a different school. How would that change the order of events?

Name

WORD SCRAMBLE

Read each sentence. Unscramble the letters in the box to make a word with the vowel sound you hear in the word *her*. Write the word to complete the sentence.

1. A huge tree stood near the _____*curve*_____ in the road.

   | v e u r c |

2. The _____*purple*_____ plums were delicious.

   | p l e r u p |

3. Mollie was _____*certain*_____ she would like the movie.

   | a c e i n r t |

4. We cooked _____*turkey*_____, rice, and carrots for dinner.

   | k e r u t y |

5. Ken's jacket was wrinkled and _____*dirty*_____.

   | r y t i d |

6. This is the _____*third*_____ time the game has been cancelled.

   | d i t h r |

7. Tim has a pet _____*turtle*_____ named Tiny.

   | l u t e r t |

8. You are the first _____*person*_____ to notice my haircut.

   | r s n o p e |

9. A _____*verse*_____ in a poem doesn't have to rhyme.

   | s r e e v |

10. I heard the _____*chirp*_____, but couldn't find the chicken.

    | r h i c p |

Think of three more words with the vowel sound you hear in *her*. Write a sentence for each word, and scramble the letters of that word. Trade papers with a partner to solve.

SORTING AND CLASSIFYING

Imagine you are writing a book report about *Little House on the Prairie*. Read the sentences below. Decide which category each belongs to and write it under that heading.

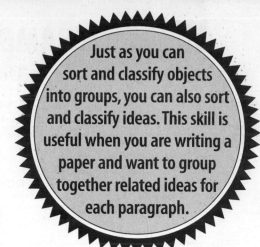

Just as you can sort and classify objects into groups, you can also sort and classify ideas. This skill is useful when you are writing a paper and want to group together related ideas for each paragraph.

> Ma pitches in by taking over the reins.
> The wagon enters the creek.
> The water rises rapidly in the creek.
> Mary is trembling and afraid.

Events that happen in the story:

1. _____ *The wagon enters the creek.* _____

_____

2. _____ *The water rises rapidly in the creek.* _____

_____

Ways the characters respond:

1. _____ *Mary trembles and is afraid.* _____

_____

2. _____ *Ma pitches in by taking over the reins.* _____

_____

Think of one more example from the story that fits each category. Write a new sentence expressing that idea. *Possible answers include: Events that happen: Jack is missing. Ways characters respond: Laura worries and feels like crying.*

IT'S A HIT!

Last year, the movie *The Gorilla's Footsteps* was a great hit!

Take a look at the poster and a newspaper review of the movie.

Then answer the question below.

THEY SCREAMED!
THEY LAUGHED!
THEY CRIED!

Miracle Films' new thriller *The Gorilla's Footsteps* will keep you on the edge of your seat. Follow the adventures of the baby gorilla as she tries to get back to her home in the rain forests of Africa after escaping from the city zoo. You'll see her deal bravely with one problem after another.

How does she do it?

What's the gorilla's secret?

You'll have to see the movie to find out for yourself.

Why do you think so many people liked this movie?

Students may write that people

liked the movie because it is a thriller that "kept them on the edge of their seats." They

may think people would enjoy a story about an animal trying to find her way home.

MAKE THE NEXT POSTER

Now you're working on gorilla movie number two! Design a poster advertising the next *Gorilla's Footsteps* movie. You'll need to give the movie a title. Also include a few sentences from a review. Remember, you want people who liked the first movie to come see the second!

Draw your poster in the space below.

Students' posters should show that the second movie
is of the same genre, and features
the same character as the first movie.

HOPPING SENTENCES

Use the words in the box to complete the sentences below.

field trip: a trip away from the classroom to learn about something

habitat: the place where an animal or plant naturally lives or grows

landscape: a view or scene of surrounding land

praying mantis: a green insect that has long stick-like legs and a triangle-shaped head and is related to the grasshopper

stalking: following closely behind someone or something without being seen

1. The animals and plants live in a hot, dry _____*habitat*_____.

2. Ms. Frizzle noticed a small green _____*praying mantis*_____ hopping on a leaf.

3. The _____*landscape*_____ of trees and mountains was beautiful.

4. The cat hiding behind the door was _____*stalking*_____ the beetle.

5. Our class went on a _____*field trip*_____ to the museum.

Choose an animal that you would like as a pet. Then write about an adventure you go on with this pet. Use at least four words from the box.

TELEVISION SCRIPT: SCREEN DIRECTIONS

Work with a partner to write a page for a TV script that includes screen directions. Plan your script below.

Characters:

Setting:

What will happen in my scene?

Screen directions I want to use:

Will my screen directions help the actors know when and how to speak?
Do my screen directions give a clear picture of the setting and action?

WHAT A SERIES!

Some of the characters in the Magic School Bus books are based on real people. Would you believe that Ms. Frizzle is like some real teachers that Joanna Cole and Bruce Degen knew? And Cole says that Arnold is really a lot like her.

Now it's your turn to create a great character based on someone you know. It can even be you. Give your character a name and then describe him or her. Draw a picture that shows what the character looks like, too.

Students' responses will vary.

Character's name: Age:

Kind of person character is:

What the character does:

ALL ABOARD

1. What parts of "The Magic School Bus Hops Home" are realistic?

The children are realistic; the science

information is factual.

2. List two things that happen in "The Magic School Bus Hops Home" that are make-believe or fantasy.

The trip to the frog habitat, the school bus turning into a frog, and the

children shrinking are all fantasy.

3. How did Joanna Cole and Bruce Degen think of the idea for Ms. Frizzle?

Joanna Cole once had a science teacher who was like Ms. Frizzle; Bruce Degen based

Ms. Frizzle on his own teachers except for the dress designs. They are his own idea.

4. What do you think makes Ms. Frizzle memorable?

Answers should include the idea that memorable characters have interesting or

unusual personalities; they are often unique in some way—how they behave,

a special talent they have, or in their physical appearance.

APOSTROPHE/ CONTRACTIONS

Complete each sentence with a contraction made from the two words in parentheses. Write the contraction on the line.

> A contraction is a shortened form of two words. An apostrophe replaces the missing letter or letters.

1. ___*What's*___ in the package? (What is)

2. My mom says ___*it's*___ for me. (it is)

3. ___*I'm*___ so excited! (I am)

4. ___*Aren't*___ birthdays great? (Are not)

5. I ___*can't*___ wait to open my gifts. (cannot)

6. I hope my mom ___*doesn't*___ mind if I tear the wrapping paper. (does not)

7. "Be careful. ___*They're*___ very delicate," she says. (They are)

8. I ___*didn't*___ want to wait another second. (did not)

9. In fact, ___*I've*___ never been very patient. (I have)

10. I ___*don't*___ mean to keep you wondering. (do not)

11. In the box, ___*there's*___ a tiny cat family made of china. (there is)

 Imagine not using any contractions when you talk. How long do you think you could keep it up? Write what you think.

Name

IS IT FOR REAL?

Parts of "The Magic School Bus Hops Home" are realistic, and parts are fantasy, or could not happen in real life. Read the sentences below. Decide if they describe something realistic or something fantastic. Then write your answers on the lines.

Story clues can provide a lot of important information. They can also be used to double-check whether something is realistic or fantastic.

1. Wanda picks up the rock and finds that Bella is gone.

   realistic

2. Ms. Frizzle's dragonfly earrings start to spin.

   fantastic

3. Ms. Frizzle and Liz hop onto the grasshopper's back.

   fantastic

4. The bus lands in a tree.

   fantastic

5. The squirrels make their nest in a tree.

   realistic

6. Food is one of the things all plants and animals need from their habitat.

   realistic

Another animal has escaped from Ms. Frizzle's classroom. Write about a realistic or fantastic search for the animal.

CLO CLEANS HOUSE

by B. B. Boynton

Read the script. Use it to complete page 44.

[**EXTERIOR** OF AN APARTMENT BUILDING. DAYTIME.]

[**LONG SHOT** OF JENNIFER AND PAUL, WHO ARE WALKING UP THE SIDEWALK TOWARD THE BUILDING.]

PAUL

I wonder if Clo was a good dog today.

JENNIFER

I'm sure she was. She always is.

NARRATOR [VO] (VO means "voice-over")

Little do they know . . .

[**FADE** TO INTERIOR OF KITCHEN.
SFX: TRASH CAN FALLING OVER]

[**WIDE SHOT** OF CLO, UNDER THE KITCHEN TABLE. SHE IS SURROUNDED BY TRASH]

CLO [raising one ear]

My super-hearing tells me that Jennifer and Paul are on their way. I'd better clean up fast!

NARRATOR [VO]

Luckily, Clo is a very special dog. [Clo wiggles her ears at the trash can. It rights itself. Then Clo sticks her tail in the air and waves it in circles. The trash floats up from the floor into the trash can—just in time.]

JENNIFER [petting Clo]

Look, Paul, the kitchen is spotless! What a good dog!

[CU ON CLO'S FACE. SHE WINKS.]

(CU means close-up)

My questions and ideas as I read

Encourage students to use this space to record their questions and ideas as they read.

FANTASY/REALITY

Look at the script "Clo Cleans House." In the first column of the chart below, write two or more things from the script that are realistic, or could happen in real life. In the second column, write down two or more things that are fantasy, or could not happen in real life.

Look for story clues to help you tell what's realistic and what's fantasy, then double-check them with what you know.

REAL LIFE	FANTASY
Possible answers:	*Possible answers:*
1. A boy and girl are walking home together, talking about their dog.	*1. a talking dog*
2. A dog makes a big mess while its owners are out.	*2. a dog cleaning house*
3. A dog runs to greet its owner, wagging its tail.	*3. a dog with special powers*
	4. a dog winking at the camera

Write another scene for "Clo Cleans House." Think of some other "special" talents for the talented pooch.

Name

RHYMING WORDS

Read each clue. Answer it with a word that rhymes with the word beside the clue. Print the word on the line.

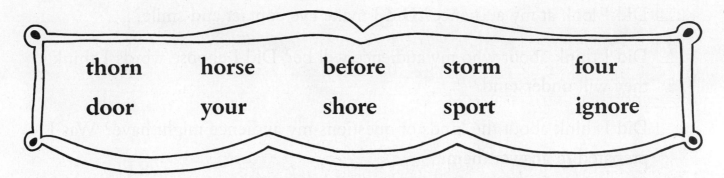

thorn	horse	before	storm	four
door	your	shore	sport	ignore

1. something you play on a field or in a gym   *sport*   port

2. rain, wind, and thunder   *storm*   form

3. the edge of a body of water   *shore*   tore

4. an entrance to a building   *door*   floor

5. pay no attention to   *ignore*   explore

6. an animal people ride   *horse*   course

7. belonging to you   *your*   pour

8. the opposite of after   *before*   adore

9. number between three and five   *four*   your

10. a sharp thing on a rose stem   *thorn*   torn

BE A BETTER SPEAKER

Use the following questions to help you be a better speaker.

☐ Did I look at my audience? Did I make eye contact and smile?

☐ Did I think about who my audience will be? Did I choose words I think they will understand?

☐ Did I think about the kinds of questions my audience might have? Was I prepared to answer them?

☐ Did I know what I was going to say and how I was going to say it?

☐ Did I practice my speech in front of a mirror?

☐ Did I use body language to help my audience understand me better?

☐ Did I remember to relax and speak slowly and clearly?

WHEN AND WHY DO I NEED TO SPEAK?	HOW CAN I BE A BETTER SPEAKER?	WHAT ADVANTAGE WILL IT GIVE ME?
Answers will vary.		

DETECTIVE PUZZLE

Complete the crossword puzzle. Use the word in the magnifying glass that fits each clue.

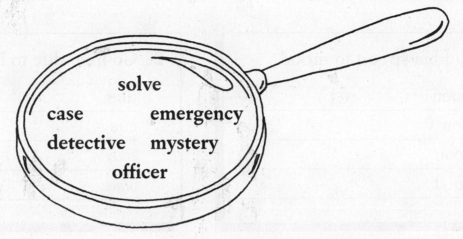

solve

case   emergency

detective   mystery

officer

ACROSS

3. a sudden and surprising situation that must be handled quickly

5. to find the answer to a problem

6. a crime investigated by a detective or a police officer

DOWN

1. a member of a police department

2. a person who follows clues to solve a crime

4. a story containing a puzzle that has to be solved

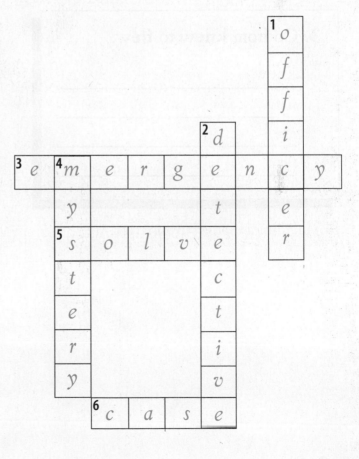

Use three of the words in the magnifying glass to write a description for a detective.

WORD LADDERS

Write each word. Change only one letter at a time. One is done for you.

1. Go from **spoon** to **mood**.

   spoon _____

   soon _____

   moon _____

   mood _____

2. Go from **due** to **blue**.

   due _____

   cue _____

   clue _____

   blue _____

3. Go from **knew** to **flew**.

   knew _____

   new _____

   few _____

   flew _____

4. Go from **tool** to **loop**.

   tool _____

   cool _____

   coop _____

   loop _____

Annotations are possible answers.

 Create your own word ladder. Trade with a partner and write the words.

MYSTERY

You will write the opening to a mystery story that sets up a puzzle to solve. Fill in the puzzle pieces below with details to help you plan the opening of your story.

The Mystery I Want to Solve

The Suspects

Detective's Name and Description

The Clues

The Setting

Is my mystery based on a problem that needs solving?

Are my characters believable?

It's No Mystery to Me

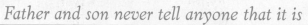

1. Encyclopedia Brown and his father trust each other.
   What details support this statement?

   Father and son never tell anyone that it is

   Encyclopedia who solves the crimes. They both keep their secret.

2. What problem do both Mr. Hunt and Mr. Xippas have?

   They both say that they own Jimbo.

3. What clues does Encyclopedia use to help solve the crime?

   He uses the dates April 1 and Friday, April 13, as clues.

4. If you can give Encyclopedia a different nickname, what might it be? Why?

   Possible answers: Three-Minute Detective; L.B. Secret I; L.B. Brain.

   Answers should be supported with statements like he solves crimes

   quickly; no one knows he's the crime-solver; he is very knowledgeable.

5. How are the Encyclopedia Brown series and the I Spy series similar?

   Answers should include the idea that both series are mysteries,

   and that the reader or viewer can use the clues provided to solve the mystery.

QUOTATION MARKS

A. Use quotation marks to show the speaker's words.

> Quotation marks (" ") show the words of a speaker. They go before the speaker's first word. They also go after the punctuation mark that follows the speaker's

"Hi. Do you have anything I can play with?" asked the wind.

1. "You can't play with my kite," said the boy.
2. "That wind is blowing too hard!" shouted the kite.
3. "I feel some string wrapped around my trunk," said the tree.
4. "This is fun!" cried the wind.
5. "I don't agree," moaned the kite.

B. What do you think the wind, the boy, the kite, or the tree might say next? Write two more quotation sentences like the ones above. Remember to include a comma, exclamation mark, or other punctuation mark after the speaker's last word.

6. _____ *Sentences will vary.* _____

   _____

7. _____

   _____

Write a dialogue between a child and a talking tree. Use quotation marks.

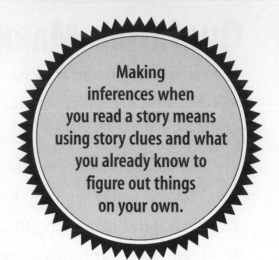

YOU CAN'T FOOL ME

Identify the correct inference in each of the following questions. Circle the letter next to the correct answer.

Making inferences when you read a story means using story clues and what you already know to figure out things on your own.

1. When Chief Brown talked about a Friday the 13th of seventeen years ago, his son Encyclopedia figured out that
   a. the date had something to do with a case.
   b. the family was going to have bad luck.
   c. it was Jimbo the Elephant's birthday.

2. When Mr. Hunt found an elephant in his yard, he thought it was a prank because
   a. elephants never forget.
   b. the police put it there.
   c. it was April Fools' Day.

3. Encyclopedia closed his eyes to do his deepest thinking and then opened them suddenly because
   a. he was puzzled.
   b. he had a memory like an elephant.
   c. he figured out the mystery.

4. You know that Encyclopedia is probably a very smart boy because

   Answers will vary.

   _____

   _____

 Explain in your own words how Encyclopedia solved the case.

THE CASE OF THE BIRTHDAY PRESENT

by Mary Hsu

Read the story. Use it to complete page 54.

Today is my birthday, and I know Mom and Dad are up to something. Yesterday I saw them in the living room whispering to each other. They stopped talking as soon as they saw me. I'll find out what they're up to. They don't call me "Smart Sally" for nothing.

During breakfast, I heard Dad whispering the name "Ike" to Mom. Ike is my best friend. Ike probably knows what the plans are for my birthday. I'll go ask him.

Wait! There's Norman, my older brother, carrying a new, long chain with a lock. Why does he need a new chain? Boy, I wish I had a bike that I could chain up! And here comes a delivery man with a big package for Dad. I can just make out the word "speed" on the box. I call Mom. She sees the delivery man in the driveway.

"What are we getting?" I ask.

"It's a computer. Your father needs one so he can do homework on weekends," she replies.

"Oh," I say. But she can't fool me! It has to be my birthday present.

I go over to Ike's house, but he isn't there. No clues to my birthday present there. So I rush home to get my present. It was just what I thought!

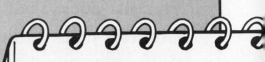

 My questions and ideas as I read

Encourage students to use this space to record their questions and ideas as they read.

MAKE INFERENCES

The author of "The Case of the Birthday Present" doesn't tell you what Sally's present is. Use story clues and what you already know to figure out what she got.

> Use story clues, along with what you already know, to help you figure out what the author doesn't tell you.

Story Clues

Dad whispers "Ike."
Norman has a chain and lock.
The word "speed" is on the box.

+

What I Know

Ike sounds like bike.
Bikes have chains and locks.
Bikes have different speeds.

=

What I Can Figure Out

Sally's present is a _____*bike*_____.

I know this because _____*the clues and what I know lead to that inference*_____.

Why do you think the main character in the story is called "Smart Sally"? What clues can you use from the story to help you figure this out?

Name

WORD SEARCH

Find each word in the puzzle below and circle it.

afternoon	true	mew
room	too	chew
moose	blue	dew

a	f	t	e	r	n	o	o	n
d	s	r	o	o	m	f	b	b
e	d	u	g	w	o	r	l	l
w	m	e	w	u	o	h	o	u
v	k	p	s	f	s	e	o	e
t	o	o	c	h	e	w	o	m

 Choose one word from each group above.
Use it in a sentence.

FIND IT AT THE LIBRARY/MEDIA CENTER

A. Suppose you want to find the following information at the library/media center. What kind of source would you look for? Write: **book, audiocassette, video, magazine,** or **CD-ROM.**

1. a recorded version of *Encyclopedia Brown Lends a Hand*

   audiocassette

2. computer game of *I Spy*

   CD-ROM

3. another mystery to read

   book

4. a TV show about elephants

   video

5. an article about Walter Wick

   magazine

B. Suppose you are searching for information on the computerized card catalog. Write **subject, author,** or **title** for the kind of search you would use.

6. A video titled *Elephants in Africa and India*

   title

7. A nonfiction book about types of calendars

   subject

8. An audiocassette called *Music from TV Shows*

   title

9. More books by Robert Blake

   author

10. More information about photographers

   subject

BUILD A CHARACTER

Meet the newest character in your own hit series. It is a space alien, and you can make it serious or silly. Does it belong in a book, a comic strip, a movie, or something else? You decide.

Add to the picture, giving your character clothes, tools, a home, and an environment. Then write a short paragraph that describes why your character belongs in a book, comic strip, or whatever place you choose.

The details of costume and

environment should work together to form a coherent character.

FILL IN THE DETAILS

Use the drawing of the space alien, and your imagination, to answer these questions:

1. What is your character's name?

2. What kind of hit series is your character in?

3. Where does your character live?

4. What other characters are in the series?

5. Is your character serious or silly? Does it dance? sing? run? climb trees?

6. What types of food does your character eat?

7. How old is this character?

8. On another sheet of paper, write about the funniest or scariest time in your character's day.

All the written information should support the character in the drawing.

I Saw It at the Fair

Read the words and their definitions. Then use the words to fill in the web.

complicated: not easy to understand or do

demonstrate: to show clearly or to explain

exhibits: things shown publicly

participants: people who join others in an activity

project: a special study, task, or activity

table: a piece of furniture with a flat top supported by legs

WHAT PEOPLE MAKE:

exhibits

project

HOW THINGS MAY APPEAR:

complicated

SCIENCE FAIR

THINGS PEOPLE DO:

demonstrate

PEOPLE YOU SEE THERE:

participants

WHERE THE PROJECTS ARE:

table

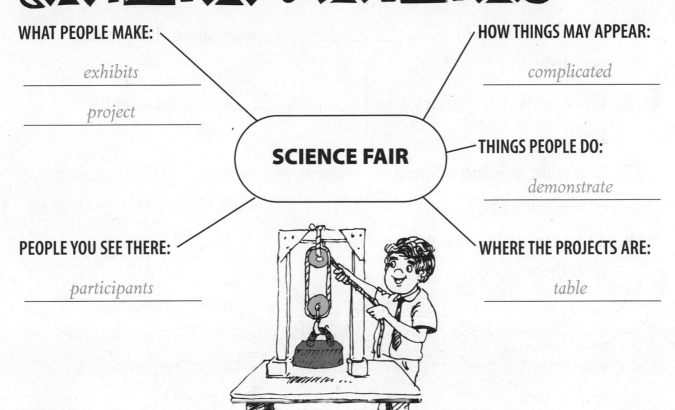

 Describe a science-fair project that you would like to do. Use as many of the words from the box as you can.

Name

THE SCIENCE FAIR

Read each sentence and the underlined word or words. Then complete the sentence with a word that has a similar meaning to the underlined word. Each sentence is completed with a word with /âr/ spelled *air* or *are*.

1. Jackie did a project for the science _____*fair*_____. show

2. He planned to give a demonstration of a _____*rare*_____ volcano. not seen often

3. Would the flow of lava _____*scare*_____ the viewers? frighten

4. Jackie set up his exhibit with _____*care*_____. attention

5. He worked hard to _____*prepare*_____ a speech about his project. get ready

6. His friends thought Jackie had a _____*flair*_____ for science. talent

7. When the volcano erupted, everyone began to _____*stare*_____ in amazement. look

8. They were glad Jackie wanted to _____*share*_____ his experiment with them. divide

Copyright © Scholastic Inc.

WHAT DOES IT MEAN?

Read each sentence about the story. Write what you infer.

1. The Rodowskys made a beeline for the World of Volcanic Activity exhibit.

   They wanted to show Jackie their interest and support.

2. Squirt stayed home with Aunt Cecilia.

   Squirt is too young to attend the school science fair.

3. Jessi didn't allow Jackie to light the match.

   Jessi cares about Jackie's safety.

4. The judges nodded and smiled during Jackie's speech.

   They were impressed.

5. The judges walked on to the last project without telling Jackie, "Good work," or "Nice going."

   In the end, they were not satisfied with Jackie's presentation.

A PERSUASIVE LETTER

Prepare to convince a friend that your favorite series should be on the Century of Greatest Hits time line. List at least three opinions you have about your favorite series. Next to each opinion, write a fact or reason that supports it.

Name of My Favorite Series:	
Opinions	**Supporting Facts/Reasons**

Did I consider my friend's interests? Did I think of all of the series' outstanding features? Did I support my opinions with convincing facts?

AN EXPLOSIVE STORY

Jackie, from the story *Jessi's Baby-sitter*, is being interviewed for a newspaper story about his science fair. What would he say?

Possible answers:

Reporter: Where did the science fair take place?

Jackie: It took place at my school, Stoneybrook Elementary.

Reporter: What was your project?

Jackie: *"Welcome to the World of Volcanic Activity"*

Reporter: What happened when you demonstrated your project?

Jackie: *My helper, Jessi, lit the match, and everyone stood back.*

Then the volcano erupted, and gooey stuff that was supposed to

be lava flowed down the side.

Reporter: What was one of the questions the judges asked?

Jackie: *One judge asked me how the crater of a volcano is created.*

Reporter: What was your answer?

Jackie: *I didn't know the answer to that question.*

Reporter: What was your prize?

Jackie: *an honorable mention*

Reporter: What did you learn from this experience?

Jackie: *I learned that I should do things by myself, and*

that I shouldn't take so much help from others.

IRREGULAR VERBS

Complete the word puzzle by writing the past tense of the irregular verbs listed below.

> Irregular verbs change in spelling when they describe an action in the past.

Clues

Across

3. past tense of *begin*
4. past tense of *sit*
5. past tense of *do*
6. past tense of *ring*

Down

1. past tense of *go*
2. past tense of *say*
4. past tense of *sing*
6. past tense of *run*

Write your own word puzzle using irregular verbs. Give it to a partner to complete.

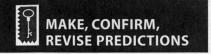

Name

WHAT DO YOU PREDICT?

Read the predictions from *Jessi's Baby-sitter*.
Then read the questions about the predictions.
Circle your answers.

> To make a prediction is to say what might happen next in a story. Predictions help readers keep track of what they're reading.

Prediction 1

Jackie will have trouble answering the judges' questions.

Which clue from the story helps you make this prediction?

a. Jackie had trouble giving his speech to two girls at the fair.

b.) Jackie had trouble answering the girls' questions at the fair.

c. Jackie knew his volcano would not explode.

What do you already know that helps you make this prediction?

a.) People have to be ready to answer questions.

b. Judges never ask questions.

c. You never have to explain your project.

Prediction 2

Jackie will not win a prize at the fair.

Which clue from the story helps you make this prediction?

a.) The judges did not tell Jackie "Good work" or "Nice going."

b. The volcano explosion did not impress the judges.

c. Jackie couldn't remember his speech.

What do you already know that helps you make this prediction?

a. Prizes are not awarded for projects that use fire.

b.) Prizewinners at a science fair can explain their projects.

c. Only projects using electricity win prizes.

 What do you think Jackie will do next year at the science fair?

DELBERT GOES TO A PARTY

by Larry Baldes

Read the story up to the (STOP) sign. Go to page 67. Then come back and finish the story.

"Come on, Delbert!" I yelled. "Let's get this bath over with. I'm already late to Kyle's swim party."

It's not easy to get a hundred-pound dog into a washtub. You have to do it paw by paw. When Delbert was finally in the tub, I squirted him with the hose and began to scrub his face with shampoo. Things were going fine until Mrs. Garcia let her cat out.

(STOP) Go to page 67.

When Delbert saw Tito, he jumped out of the tub and ran toward the cat. He flew into Mrs. Garcia's yard. His eyes were wild and his face was full of foam. "Mad dog!" she screamed. "Stop him before he hurts Tito!"

Delbert chased Tito. I chased Delbert. Mrs. Garcia yelled, "Run, Tito, run! Stop that dog!"

Tito ran into Kyle's backyard and hid. Delbert charged into the yard. When he saw Kyle's friends in the swimming pool, he forgot about Tito. He jumped into the pool and paddled around, lapping at the water.

It wasn't easy getting Delbert out of the pool. I had just dragged him back home when Mom arrived.

"Well," she said to Delbert, "I see we've had a nice bath!" Mom gave me an extra two dollars for doing such a good job. I gave one of the dollars to Kyle.

My questions and ideas as I read

Encourage students to use this space to record their questions and ideas as they read.

Copyright © Scholastic Inc.

MAKE, CONFIRM, REVISE PREDICTIONS

Look at the chart for "Delbert Goes to a Party." Fill in the empty boxes with story clues, what you know, and what you think will happen.

When you make a prediction, think about what might happen next in a story. A prediction is based on story clues and what you already know.

STORY CLUES	WHAT I KNOW	WHAT I THINK WILL HAPPEN
Delbert is a big dog.	Bathing a big dog is not easy.	*Possible answer: Delbert will get out of the tub.*
Mrs. Garcia lets her cat out.	*Possible answer: Dogs like to chase cats.*	Delbert will chase Tito.
There's going to be a swim party.	Most dogs like to swim.	*Possible answer: Delbert will get his bath in the pool.*

Now go back to page 66 and finish the story.

How many of your predictions were correct? _____

What do you think will happen during Delbert's next bath? Write a sentence about, or draw a picture of, your guess.

Name

THOSE HIT CHARACTERS!

Read each sentence. Unscramble the word in parentheses and write it on the line. Underline the letters that make the /âr/ sound.

1. Peter Rabbit is a rabbit, not a ____h<u>are</u>____. **(raeh)**

2. Babar has a ____fl<u>air</u>____ for dressing. **(alrfi)**

3. If you owned Snoopy or Lassie, you wouldn't need this sign: "____B<u>e</u>w<u>are</u>____ of Dog." **(wrBeea)**

4. Clifford's red coat is a ____r<u>are</u>____ color for a dog. **(arer)**

5. Ms. Frizzle has red ____h<u>air</u>____. **(ihra)**

6. Some might say Amelia Bedelia is ____squ<u>are</u>____, or not cool. **(erasqu)**

7. You'll rarely find Encyclopedia Brown relaxing in a ____ch<u>air</u>____. **(rahic)**

8. Iktomi can ____b<u>are</u>ly____ wait to try his tricks! **(lyarbe)**

9. The baby-sitters really ____c<u>are</u>____ about children. **(erca)**

10. Madeline is a very ____f<u>air</u>____ French schoolgirl. **(arfi)**

Copyright © Scholastic Inc.

READING GRAPHIC AIDS

Use the time line, bar graph, and calendar to answer the questions.

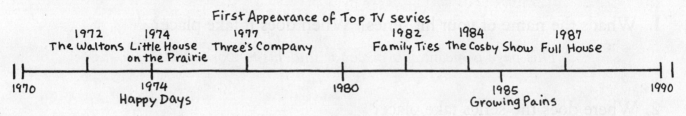

First Appearance of Top TV series

1972	1974	1977	1982	1984	1987
The Waltons	Little House on the Prairie	Three's Company	Family Ties	The Cosby Show	Full House

1970 — 1974 Happy Days — 1980 — 1985 Growing Pains — 1990

1. What does the time line show? _It shows when top TV series first appeared on the screen._

2. What two TV series made their first appearance the same year? What year was that?

"Little House on the Prairie" and "Happy Days" both made their first appearance in 1974.

3. What does the bar graph show? _It shows how many people voted for their favorite TV series._

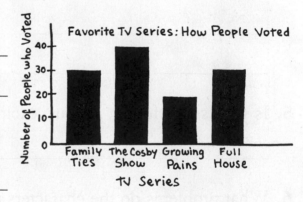

Favorite TV Series: How People Voted

4. Which two TV shows got the same number of votes? How many votes did they each get? _"Family Ties" and "Full House" each got 30 votes._

5. One week after the 20th, a rerun of "The Waltons" will be shown. What date is that? What day of the week is it? _It is March 27th — a Saturday._

MARCH						
Sun.	Mon.	Tue.	Wed.	Thu.	Fri.	Sat.
	1	2	3	4	5	6
7	8	9	10	11	12	13
14	15	16	17	18	19	20
21	22	23	24	25	26	27
28	29	30	31			

6. A new TV show will be broadcast on the third Wednesday of the month. What date is that? _It is March 17th._

NOTE THE ELEMENTS OF YOUR SERIES

Use this page to help you organize information about your hit series.

1. What's the name of your hit series? When does it take place?

   This page is meant as a place for students to work out their ideas.
   _____

2. Where does the series take place?

   _____
   _____

3. Who are the main characters?

   _____
   _____
   _____

4. How do the main characters get along with one another?

   _____
   _____

5. Is your series funny, serious, exciting, or scary?

   _____

6. What problems do the characters need to solve during your episode?

   _____
   _____
   _____

7. Are you going to add any new characters in this episode? If so, describe them.

   _____
   _____

STORYBOARD YOUR EPISODE

Think about what's going to happen during this episode of your series.

Fill in the storyboard, using words or drawings to show what happens in each scene.

This page is meant as a place for students to work out their ideas.

WRITING A CONVERSATION

Write a conversation between two characters from two different selections. Make the conversation sound natural. In the chart below, make notes about your conversation. Use your notes to help you write your dialogue.

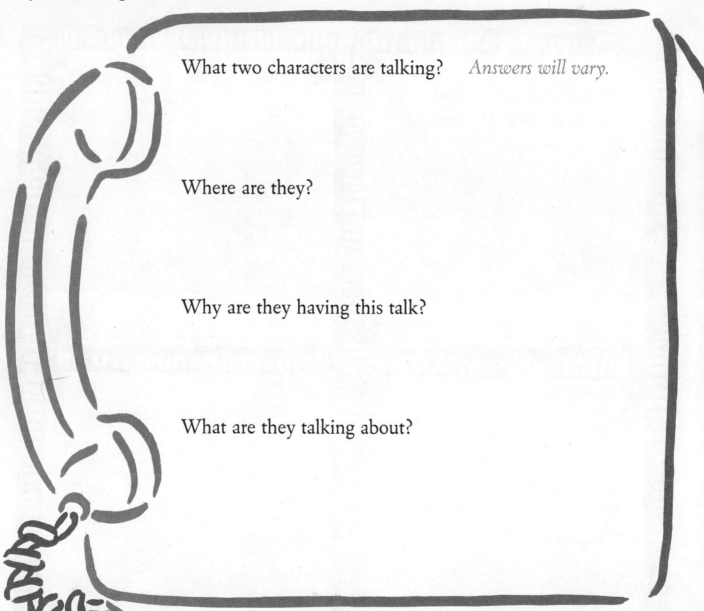

What two characters are talking?   *Answers will vary.*

Where are they?

Why are they having this talk?

What are they talking about?

Will my characters talk like real people?

Will the dialogue help the reader know what the characters are like?

READER'S LOG

Keep track of books you read about creative expression. When you've finished the unit, look over your list. Which book did you like best? Why?

Book Title	Author	Genre	Connection to Creative Expression
Answers will vary.			

My favorite book: _____

Reasons why I like this book best: _____

_____

WHAT DID I LEARN?

1. What are the steps involved in making a book?

   Students should include the basic steps: planning a book, writing the words,

   making the pictures, editing the words, making sure it all fits together, printing it.

2. Describe the different jobs that are necessary to create a book.

   Students might mention editing, copy editing, designing, and illustrating.

3. What do you think is the most difficult part about making a book?

   Answers will relate to the students' experiences.

4. On another sheet of paper, draw a picture or write about something you did in the Publishing Company.

   Students' responses should be specific to an activity they did
   in the learning center.

BE A BETTER READER

Use the following questions to help you be a better reader.

☐ Do I read something every day?

☐ Do I try to make a picture in my mind while I read? Do I ask myself, "How do the characters look? How does the setting look?"

☐ Do I shift the speed at which I read, depending on my purpose for reading and the type of book it is?

☐ Do I make connections between what I read and my own life. Do I look for experiences I've had myself in my reading?

WHY DO I NEED TO READ?	HOW CAN I BE A BETTER READER?	WHAT ADVANTAGE WILL IT GIVE ME?
Entries will vary.		

STORY EVENTS   *Answers will vary.*

Story Title _____

Write or draw the story events in the order that they occur.

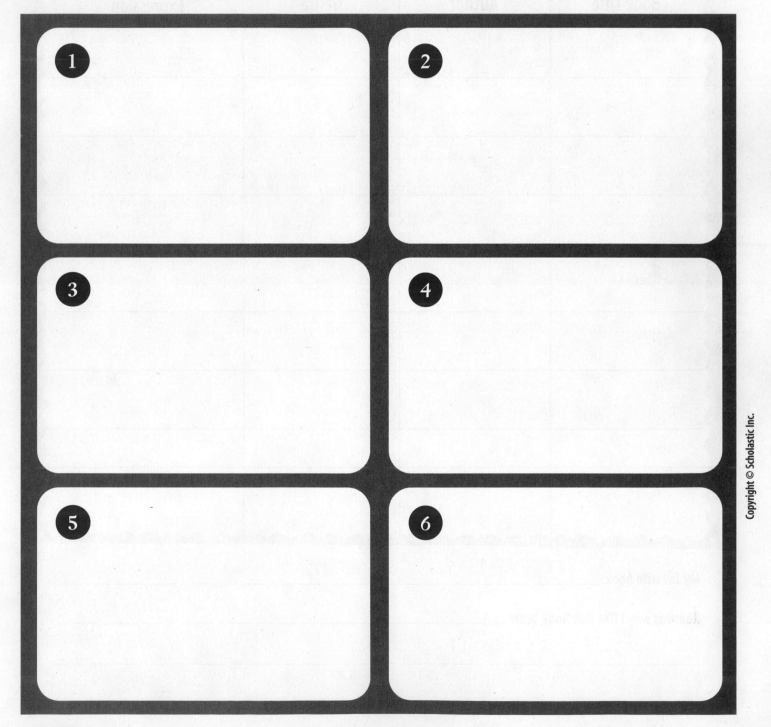

★ NEWSLETTER ★

Welcome to *Time Detectives*

A dish in your grandmother's cupboard, a photo in an album, an old trunk stored in the basement—what do these things have in common? They're clues to the past. In your Anthology you'll see how clues can be pieced together to form a picture of life long ago. Who knows what you'll "dig up" while you're reading?

Meet the Time Detectives

Decide for yourself what really happened and what was imagined. You'll read a story about a family that finds artifacts from the past.

+PLUS+ **Read on and you'll meet some kids who are real "dirt detectives." See what they're learning about their hometown's history.**

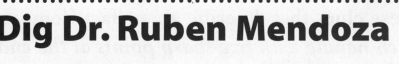

Dig Dr. Ruben Mendoza

Learn to dig the past with Dr. Ruben Mendoza. With this exciting archaeologist, you'll discover how artifacts can tell you about life long ago.

Look at the Clues

Clues to the past—that's what this picture dictionary is about. You'll read about all kinds of artifacts—from *A* to *Z*. In a photo biography by Diane Hoyt-Goldsmith, you'll see how Native Americans pass stories from grandparents to grandchildren.

★ NEWSLETTER ★

Add Up the Evidence

You'll put together a picture of the past when you read *Wild and Woolly Mammoths* by Aliki. Then you'll read a story within a story about a tornado. You'll also read two poems about the weather. Finally, you'll jump into the future, where kids find something very unusual—a book!

+PLUS+ Discover what third graders think will happen in the future.

Let's Visit an Archaeological Site

It's dusty and dirty, but it can also be one of the most exciting places on Earth. You can't imagine what you might dig up here.

Things You'll Do

How will you describe something you use every day? Put it all on the **artifact card**. Look carefully. There are lots of **picture clues** to be found in old photographs. What things will describe you, your family, and even your neighborhood? Put them in your own **time capsule**.

Getting Started

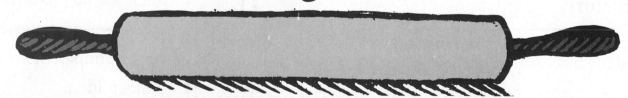

The year is 2110. Read these clues that describe an artifact from your life: *silvery object, four-inch handle with five sharp points at the end, easily held in one hand, maybe used for picking up things.*

Did you guess that these clues describe a fork? Well, you're right. Try writing clues for another artifact in your house. Ask someone to guess which artifact you are describing.

WELCOME TO THE ARCHAEOLOGICAL SITE

1. How do you think people learn about the distant past?

Students' answers might include studying prehistoric

artifacts or examining ancient ruins.

2. What do you think you could find out from the ruins of old buildings?

Possible answers: finding out what the building was used for,

when it was built, or what kind of people used it

3. What do you want to know about what archaeologists do?

Students might want to know how archaeologists know

where to dig or how many artifacts they might find in a day.

4. How can you find out more about archaeologists?

Students might suggest writing letters to an archaeologist

or looking up information in the library.

STUDENT LOG

Here's a way to keep track of what you do at the Archaeological Site.

Fill in the chart when you visit the Archaeological Site.

Date	What I Did	What I Learned
	Students' entries will vary.	

Copyright © Scholastic Inc.

CLUES IN THE DIRT

Use the words from the box to complete the archaeologist's notes.

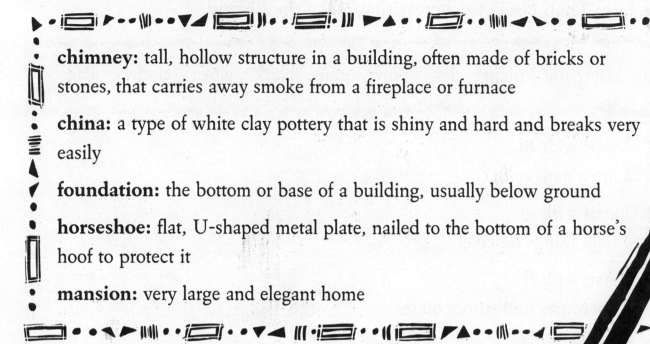

chimney: tall, hollow structure in a building, often made of bricks or stones, that carries away smoke from a fireplace or furnace

china: a type of white clay pottery that is shiny and hard and breaks very easily

foundation: the bottom or base of a building, usually below ground

horseshoe: flat, U-shaped metal plate, nailed to the bottom of a horse's hoof to protect it

mansion: very large and elegant home

ARCHAEOLOGIST'S NOTES:

1. The tall brick _____chimney_____ is badly damaged.

2. Only three sides of the _____foundation_____ are left below the ground.

3. Near the chimney, there is a small _____china_____ doll. Its head has a tiny crack over the right eye.

4. I found a rusted _____horseshoe_____ with one nail missing.

5. I think the house was a _____mansion_____, because the foundation looks very large.

 Make a drawing to go along with the archaeologist's notes.
Label your drawing.

l-BLENDS

Find a word from the box that fits each clue below. Write the word on the line. Then circle the letters that make the *l*-blend.

blast   fly   plant   claw   plow   glue   black   glove   clothes   flag

1. I start with **bl**.
   I am a dark color. _____black_____

2. I start with **gl**.
   I hold things together. _____glue_____

3. I start with **fl**.
   I have stars and stripes on me. _____flag_____

4. I start with **cl**.
   You wear me every day. _____clothes_____

5. I start with **bl**.
   I am a loud noise. _____blast_____

6. I start with **pl**.
   A farmer uses me. _____plow_____

7. I start with **fl**.
   I am an insect. _____fly_____

8. I start with **pl**.
   I have green leaves. _____plant_____

9. I start with **gl**.
   I keep your hand warm. _____glove_____

10. I start with **cl**.
    I am very sharp. _____claw_____

DESCRIPTION: SENSORY DETAILS

Think of a place you know like a store or a park. Write a description of it. Picture the place in your mind. Include details to describe it—sights, voices and other sounds, smells, and the feel of things you can touch. Use the chart below to plan your writing.

THE PLACE I WANT TO DESCRIBE

What do I see?

Students' responses will vary.

What do I hear?

What do I smell?

What do I touch?

Have I used lots of details to describe a place?

Do my details make readers feel as if they are visiting the place?

Are there any other details I can add?

There's No Place Like Home

1. *Home Place* is a story-within-a-story. Write a sentence telling what each story is about.

   Possible response: In the first story a family takes a walk in the woods and

   finds the ruins of a house. The second story is about the family that lived

   in the house long ago.

2. How does the girl figure out what the people who lived in the house might have been like?

   Possible response: The girl uses artifacts, or the old objects that she finds,

   to imagine who the people in the house were and how they lived.

3. The girl in *Home Place* is a kind of "dirt detective" like George and AnnMarie. How are they alike? How are they different?

   The girl in Home Place *is looking for clues in the ruins.*

   The dirt detectives also dig through ruins. The girl uses her imagination

   to think about what happened. The dirt detectives use scientific tools.

4. Do you think the girl in *Home Place* would enjoy going on a dig with George and AnnMarie? Why or why not?

   Possible response: The girl is very interested in the home site she has discovered, and

   would probably enjoy learning about the tools that archaeologists use.

SUBJECT/VERB AGREEMENT

Complete each sentence by choosing the correct form of the verb in parentheses ( ). Write it on the line.

> A present-tense verb must agree with the subject of a sentence. If the subject is singular, the verb must also be singular. If the subject is plural, the verb must also be plural.

1. Tom _____*feels*_____ something! (feel, feels)

2. They _____*need*_____ to be careful. (need, needs)

3. It _____*sounds*_____ as if it is made of metal. (sound, sounds)

4. Jill _____*wants*_____ to see it. (want, wants)

5. It _____*looks*_____ like a strange contraption. (look, looks)

6. Tom and Jill _____*put*_____ it together. (put, puts)

7. Suddenly, Tom _____*knows*_____ what it is. (know, knows)

8. He _____*tells*_____ Jill it is an old bicycle. (tell, tells)

9. Jill _____*asks*_____ if they can fix it. (ask, asks)

10. Both Jill and Tom _____*think*_____ it would be fun to try to fix it. (think, thinks)

 Write three sentences about something you and a friend like to do. Use present-tense verbs. Check to see that the verb agrees with the subject of each sentence.

CIRCLE IT

Read the sentences about *Home Place*. Circle
a conclusion that can be drawn from the sentences.
Write your own conclusion for the last example.

Use story clues
and what you already
know to draw conclusions,
or come up with a new
idea about the
story event.

1. Papa washes dishes. Mama sweeps the floor.
   Uncle Ferd shuts up the chickens for the night.
   a. Papa doesn't like to sweep the floor.
   b. There are plenty of chores to be done.
   c. Uncle Ferd is Mama's brother.

2. The swing hangs vacant in the black walnut tree, listless in the heat. Uncle
   Ferd wipes the sweat from his forehead. Someone swats at a mosquito.
   a. The swing is broken.
   b. It is a windy autumn day.
   c. It is a hot and windless summer day.

3. There's thunder and lightning. Tommy sleeps straight through the storm.
   a. Tommy is a light sleeper.
   b. Tommy is a heavy sleeper.
   c. Tommy is afraid of storms.

4. The dry dusty earth soaks up the water. The roots of the plants drink it up. A
   small green snake coils happily in the wet woods.

   The rain is badly needed.

   _____

   _____

STONE AGE SECRETS

by Tonya Leslie from SCHOLASTIC NEWS

Read the article. Use it to complete page 88.

When Jean-Marie Chauvet shone his flashlight on the dark wall of the cave, he was not prepared to see animals in the flickering light. But there on the wall were pictures of 300 beasts! There was a parade of panthers, owls, bears, and other animals. Some animals were painted alone. Other animals were painted together and looked like they were fighting.

Chauvet works with the French government to protect historic caves. He knew right away that this cave was a big discovery.

Why is the cave art so important? It is prehistoric. That means that it was created during a time called the Stone Age.

The cave paintings give clues about prehistoric life. Scientists can tell that people used colorful minerals from the earth to paint the animals different colors. By studying the art, scientists can learn more about the animals that lived back then. Many of them, like woolly rhinos and mammoths, are now extinct.

Chauvet made other discoveries in the cave. He found bones and footprints of ancient cave bears, knives made of stone, and remains of fireplaces. Scientists hope that these discoveries will add pieces to the prehistoric puzzle.

My questions and ideas as I read

Encourage students to use this space to record their questions and ideas as they read.

DRAW CONCLUSIONS

Scientists use clues to draw conclusions, or come up with ideas, about the past. The conclusions below are based on "Stone Age Secrets." Find the clue in the article that led to each conclusion, and write it in the space provided.

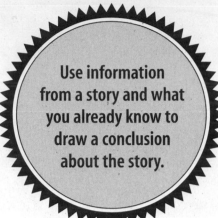

Use information from a story and what you already know to draw a conclusion about the story.

1. **Conclusion:** Prehistoric people made tools.

Clue: _____

Chauvet found knives made of stone in the cave.

2. **Conclusion:** Panthers lived in Stone Age France.

Clue: _____

Panthers were shown in the art that was found in the cave.

3. **Conclusion:** Prehistoric people knew how to create fire.

Clue: _____

Chauvet found the remains of fireplaces.

THINK & WRITE Write a short newscast for the evening news that describes Jean-Marie Chauvet's discovery.

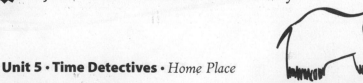

Name

Read the pairs of sentences. Write word clues for each underlined word and then write its meaning.

1. The boy used a long wooden <u>stick</u> to scratch in the dirt.

   Word clues: _____ *long, wooden* _____

   Meaning: _____ *a long, thin piece of wood* _____

   You can <u>stick</u> this picture onto the piece of paper with glue.

   Word clues: _____ *onto the piece of paper; glue* _____

   Meaning: _____ *to join one thing to another* _____

2. This <u>kind</u> of story is the type that I like best.

   Word clues: _____ *type* _____

   Meaning: _____ *a special one* _____

   The children were very <u>kind</u> to their mother and treated her well.

   Word clues: _____ *treated her well* _____

   Meaning: _____ *showing goodness or willingness to help* _____

3. The story is set <u>back</u> in time and takes place a hundred years ago.

   Word clues: _____ *time, a hundred years ago* _____

   Meaning: _____ *a time earlier than right now* _____

   Her hair hung down her <u>back</u> and almost reached her waist.

   Word clues: _____ *parts of the body: hair and waist* _____

   Meaning: _____ *the part of the body from neck to waist that is on the opposite side of your face* _____

4. Mama <u>rocks</u> back and forth in her old chair on the porch.

   Word clues: _____ *back and forth* _____

   Meaning: _____ *moves back and forth* _____

   We piled the smooth stones and larger <u>rocks</u> by the fence.

   Word clues: _____ *stones* _____

   Meaning: _____ *stones* _____

 Write one sentence using the word *light* in two different ways. Do the same thing for the word *place*.

JOT IT DOWN!

Imagine that your teacher has just asked you to write a report on what you learned about the job of a dirt detective from the article, "Meet the Dirt Detectives!" First you must take notes. Write supporting details for each main idea below.

Reminder: A note can be a word or a phrase.

1. Tools a Dirt Detective Needs

paintbrush — for brushing away dirt

trowel — for digging

meter stick — for measuring

measuring tape — for larger objects

map — to write down details about where you dig

paper bag — to store findings

dustpan — for collecting dirt

whisk broom — for cleaning area

2. About Digging

not boring — time goes fast

need patience

full of surprises

can be dangerous — check with law officers

Now write a main idea for these details. Then add two more details.

3. _____ *Possible answer: Objects You Might Find*

old china dishes — old nails

pieces of brick

pieces of glass

Use your notes to write your report.

DIGGING UP THE PAST

Draw a line from each word on the left to its definition on the right.

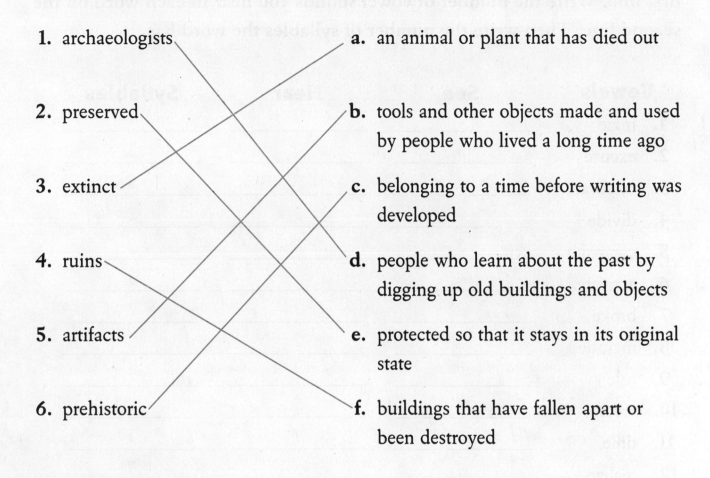

1. archaeologists

2. preserved

3. extinct

4. ruins

5. artifacts

6. prehistoric

a. an animal or plant that has died out

b. tools and other objects made and used by people who lived a long time ago

c. belonging to a time before writing was developed

d. people who learn about the past by digging up old buildings and objects

e. protected so that it stays in its original state

f. buildings that have fallen apart or been destroyed

Would you like to be an archaeologist? Write about why or why not. Use at least two of the words from the left column.

Name

SYLLABICATION: VOWEL-SILENT *e*

Say each word. Write the number of vowels you see in each word on the first line. Write the number of vowel sounds you hear in each word on the second line. Then write the number of syllables the word has.

Vowels	See	Hear	Syllables
1. froze	2	1	1
2. excuse	3	2	2
3. celebrate	4	3	3
4. divide	3	2	2
5. campsite	3	2	2
6. activate	4	3	3
7. broke	2	1	1
8. include	3	2	2
9. rule	2	1	1
10. create	3	2	2
11. time	2	1	1
12. realize	4	3	3
13. decide	3	2	2
14. organize	4	3	3

Copyright © Scholastic Inc.

DRAW CONCLUSIONS

The sentences below come from *Wild and Woolly Mammoths*. Circle a conclusion that can be drawn from the sentences. Write your own conclusions for the last example.

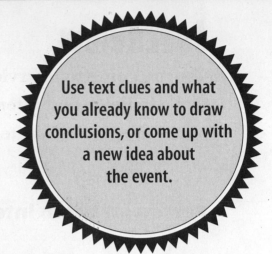

Use text clues and what you already know to draw conclusions, or come up with a new idea about the event.

1. Woolly mammoths flourished thousands of years ago. Long, long before then, when dinosaurs lived, the earth was hot and swampy.

   a. The dinosaurs lived at the same time as the woolly mammoths.

   (b.) Dinosaurs had become extinct before the time of the woolly mammoths.

   c. Woolly mammoths lived when the earth was hot and swampy.

2. There was one hunter even more dangerous to woolly mammoths than the fierce saber-toothed cat. That was the human hunter.

   a. Humans hunted the saber-toothed cat.

   b. Woolly mammoths were not in danger from the saber-toothed cat.

   (c.) Human hunters killed more woolly mammoths than saber-toothed cats were able to.

3. Mammoths traveled in peaceful herds.

   Possible answer: Mammoths did not hunt other animals.

If scientists found the remains of a woolly mammoth near your school, what conclusions would you draw? Write down your ideas.

INTERVIEW

You are going to interview a person of your choice. First, choose someone you admire or find interesting. Then, think about what you'd like to know about the person. Write questions to ask the person in the space below.

Students' responses will vary.

Person I Want to Interview:

_____

Questions That Ask *Who*, *What*, *When*, *Where*, *Why*, or *How*

Question:

Question:

Question:

Question:

Question:

Will readers get to know the person I interviewed through the questions I asked?

Have I included facts about the person?

Name

HIDDEN TREASURES

Pretend you are on an archaeological dig with Dr. Ruben Mendoza in New England. There you find a number of artifacts in a large, rectangle-shaped area. In one corner you dig up pieces of glass bottles, bits of pottery, an almost-whole plate, and a large metal soup spoon. In another corner you find pieces of cloth and a needle. On the other side of the rectangle, you find a doll's head and pieces of what look like a bed.

What do the artifacts tell you about this place? Draw what the place might have looked like when people lived here.

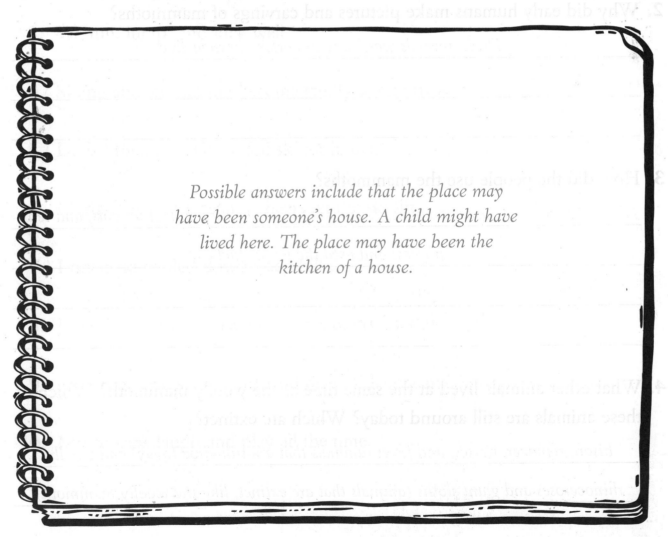

Possible answers include that the place may have been someone's house. A child might have lived here. The place may have been the kitchen of a house.

TAKE NOTES

Read the paragraphs and identify the main ideas in them. Write the main ideas in the box. Then complete the outline. Write the main topics next to Roman numerals and subtopics next to capital letters.

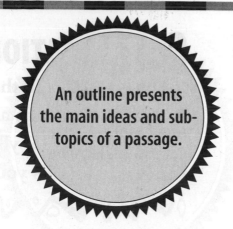

An outline presents the main ideas and sub-topics of a passage.

Fierce Cats of the Ice Age

One of the most dangerous animals that ever lived was *Smilodon*, the saber-toothed cat of North America. *Smilodon* stood 40 inches (102 cm) tall at the shoulders! It used its 9-inch (23-cm) fangs to stab its prey, slow-moving sloths and mastodons.

The biggest cat that ever lived was the cave lion, which roamed Europe during the Ice Age. This giant cat was more than a quarter larger than African lions. Like modern lions, the cave lion often hunted its prey in prides.

Answers may vary.

The Smilodon was one of the most dangerous cats in North America.

The biggest cat that ever lived was the cave lion.

Title: _Fierce Cats of the Ice Age_

   I. _Saber-toothed cat_

      A. _Lived in North America_

      B. _Stood 40 inches tall at shoulder and had 9-inch fangs_

   II. _Cave lion_

      A. _Lived in Europe_

      B. _More than a quarter larger than African lions_

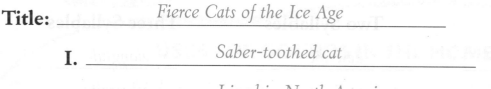

Go back and find your favorite part of *Wild and Woolly Mammoths.* Choose at least three paragraphs and outline the main topics and subtopics in them. Check off ideas you would like to further research.

FUTURE ARCHAEOLOGY

What would an archaeologist in the future think of artifacts from today? Would he or she look at a fork and think people used it to comb their hair?

Look at the objects below. For each one, explain to the museum staff how it could be used. Your explanation can be funny or serious.

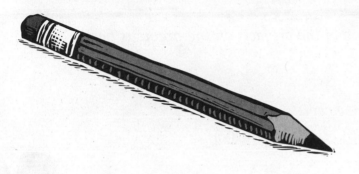

Possible response: used to push the buttons

of a tiny calculator

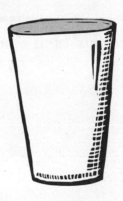

Possible response: used to hold small nails

and screws; used to

hold beverages

Possible response: used to whittle

Possible response: used to carry messages

over great distances

Copyright © Scholastic Inc.

MAKE AN EXHIBIT CARD

An exhibit card gives information about an artifact. It tells where the artifact comes from, when it was made, what it's made of, how it was used, and so on.

Look back at the artifacts on page 105. Choose one and make an exhibit card for it.

Students' cards should relate to one of the artifacts on the previous page.

Copyright © Scholastic Inc.

STRONG WIND!

Read the words and their definitions. Use the words to label the picture below.

tornado: a violent, whirling column of air

twister: a tornado

ditch: a long, narrow trench

hail: small balls of ice that fall from the sky

damage: the harm that something does

gust: a sudden, strong blast of wind

1. The weather report warned of a _____ *tornado* _____ with a huge funnel cloud.

2. A sudden _____ *gust* _____ of wind blew off my hat.

3. A long _____ *ditch* _____ that ran along the side of the road was filled with water.

4. The rain turned into icy balls of _____ *hail* _____ .

5. That _____ *twister* _____ was the worst tornado I've ever seen.

6. The storm blew over trees and caused a lot of _____ *damage* _____ .

 Use all of the vocabulary words above to write a TV news report about a bad storm.

CONSONANT BLENDS WITH S

All the words in the puzzle have consonant blends with *s*. In a consonant blend, you pronounce each letter. Choose a word from the box. Write it on the lines next to its clue. Then circle the letters that make the consonant blend with *s*.

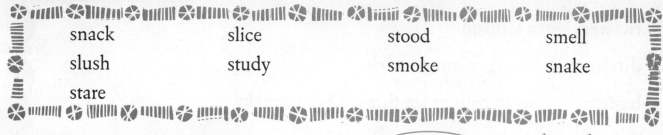

snack	slice	stood	smell
slush	study	smoke	snake
stare			

1. what you do with your nose   (s m) e l l

2. a long, hard look   (s t) a r e

3. spend time learning a subject   (s t) u d y

4. a piece cut from something larger   (s l) i c e

5. reptile with no legs   (s n) a k e

6. the opposite of sat   (s t) o o d

7. partly melted snow   (s l) u s h

8. a small, light meal   (s n) a c k

9. what comes out of a chimney   (s m) o k e

Name

PREDICTIONS

Fill in the circle beside the best answer, or write your answer on the lines.

1. To make an accurate prediction, you should:

    (a) use your prior knowledge.

    (b) use story clues.

    (c) use picture clues.

    (d) all of the above

2. When you confirm a prediction, you:

    (a) use prior knowledge.

    (b) distinguish between fantasy and reality.

    (c) find out if what you predicted actually happened in the story.

    (d) revise your original prediction.

3. Which of the following story clues in *Tornado* would not help you predict that Tornado would become a member of Pete's family?

    (a) Pete brings him food, but he won't eat.

    (b) Pete's father says, "The storm's over, and you're among friends."

    (c) Pete says, "Daddy, can we keep him? Please?"

    (d) Pete's father and the dog shake like two men striking a bargain.

4. What do you already know about people and dogs that helps you predict that Pete will become attached to Tornado?

Students may suggest that many people love dogs and that the

longer you have a dog, the closer you feel to it.

Suppose you're going to a natural history museum as part of a class trip. Write a short paragraph predicting some of the things you might see.

WRITE A FIRST-PERSON ACCOUNT

Write a first-person account. Tell about a storm that you experienced
recently. Answer the questions below to help you plan your account.

What happened to me? _____ *Answers will vary.* _____

_____

What did I see? smell? _____

_____

What did I hear? _____

_____

How did I feel? _____

_____

What did I think and do? _____

Did I tell about a storm that really happened?

Did I use the pronouns *I*, *me*, *my*, and *mine*?

Did I tell what I thought or felt?

TWISTER!

1. What is a tornado? Describe in your own words what a twister sounds like and what it can do.

   Possible answer: A tornado is a whirling, funnel-shaped column of air

   that moves across the ground. It roars and rumbles like the sound of a huge train.

   A tornado destroys things in its path.

2. What was different about the tornado that struck the family's farm and the one that struck Pete's home?

   The family saw the tornado coming and had time to get into the storm cellar.

   The tornado struck Pete's home without warning and ripped the roof off

   while they were eating lunch.

3. What clues were there that Tornado had been taught a card trick by his previous owners?

   He kept poking Pete when Pete was playing cards; he pricked his ears forward

   and looked eager; when Pete held the cards out to him, he took one in his mouth.

4. If you could give Tornado a different name, what would it be? Why?

   Students' answers may reflect what happened to Tornado,

   such as surviving the storm, or his actions.

COMPOUND SENTENCES

Rewrite the sentence pairs below to make compound sentences. One has been done for you.

> A compound sentence is made up of two simple sentences that are joined by a comma and the word *and*.

Kate made a cake. It tasted great.

Kate made a cake, and it tasted great.

1. Jim plays basketball. He coaches too.

    Jim plays basketball, and he coaches, too.

   _____

2. Mom made a wonderful dinner. We all enjoyed it.

    Mom made a wonderful dinner, and we all enjoyed it.

   _____

3. Pat made a lovely drawing. She gave it to her friend.

    Pat made a lovely drawing, and she gave it to her friend.

   _____

4. Maria speaks Spanish. She reads Spanish magazines.

    Maria speaks Spanish, and she reads Spanish magazines.

   _____

5. Dad wants to go shopping. He also wants to go to the movies.

    Dad wants to go shopping, and he also wants to go to the movies.

   _____

Write four sentences about things you and a friend did together. Then use the word *and* to combine the sentences into two compound sentences.

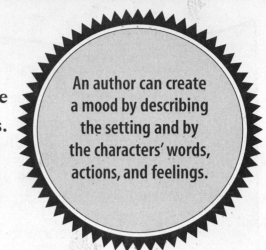

MOOD

An author can create a mood by describing the setting and by the characters' words, actions, and feelings.

MOODS

Read the sentences below from *Tornado*. Think about the descriptive details the author uses. Write the mood you think the author wants to get across.

1. The morning went by, slow and scary. We did stay close to the house. Folks didn't call our part of the country Tornado Alley for nothing.

   Mood: *Possible answers: scary, danger, worried*

2. *He took the card!* I remember it to this day. It was the three of hearts. The dog was standing there with the three of hearts in his mouth!

   Mood: *Possible answer: excitement*

3. Emma Lou came over and held out her hand. "Tornado, give me Carey's turtle. And that turtle better be all right or you'll be sorry."

   Mood: *Possible answer: anger*

4. Tornado would run around the tree one way and I'd run the other, and when we would almost bump into each other, it would make us run some more.

   Mood: *Possible answer: funny, humorous*

Write a paragraph describing an enjoyable or exciting event in your life. Use descriptive details to get the mood across.

ROLLER COASTER IN THE SKY

Read the story below. Use it to complete page 115.

The small plane buzzed along through a clear sky. Far below, the blue and green water sparkled brightly. Sara hummed in rhythm with the engine.

Then a shadow began to move across the ocean. Sara sat up alertly and leaned forward for a better view. She grasped the controls tightly in sudden fear. As she watched, she saw a huge black cloud and flashes of lightning.

Within moments, the storm struck with all its force! Rain and icy hail lashed the windows. Inside the storm cloud, it was darker than the darkest night. Strong winds tossed the little plane high, then shoved it down. "This is the wildest roller coaster ride of my life!" Sara shivered with fright.

After one last gust that made the plane rock and roll, the squall passed on. Sara pulled back on the control wheel. The nose lifted, and the plane straightened out. Sara sighed and relaxed as she eased the plane onto a level path again.

My questions and ideas as I read

Encourage students to use this space to record their questions and ideas as they read.

Copyright © Scholastic Inc.

WHAT'S THE MOOD?

Read each question about the mood. Write your answers on the lines.

1. What is the mood of the story in the first paragraph? What are the clues?

   Mood: _calm, peaceful_

   Clues: _clear sky, water sparkled_

2. What is the mood of the story in the second paragraph? What are the clues?

   Mood: _worry, danger_

   Clues: _shadow, grasped the controls, tightly, flashes of lightning,_

   huge black cloud

3. What is the mood of the story in the third paragraph? What are the clues?

   Mood: _scary, frightening_

   Clues: _storm struck with all its force; rain and hail lashed against the_

   windows, shivered with fright

4. What is the mood of the story in the last paragraph? What are the clues?

   Mood: _relieved_

   Clues: _The nose lifted. Sara sighed and relaxed; she eased the plane onto a_

   level path again.

Imagine that you are Sara being interviewed about your experience by a TV reporter. Write your answer to the question "How did you feel when you were inside the storm?"

CONSONANT BLENDS WITH s

Some words, such as *snake* and *storm* have consonant blends with *s*.
Choose a word from the box that completes each pair below. Circle the
letters that make up the blend.

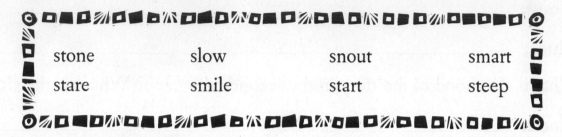

| stone | slow | snout | smart |
| stare | smile | start | steep |

Write words that are opposites.

1. frown or _____ (sm)ile

2. _____ (st)art _____ or stop

3. fast or _____ (sl)ow

4. flat or _____ (st)eep

Write words that are synonyms, or alike in meaning.

5. rock, pebble, _____ (st)one

6. bright, intelligent, _____ (sm)art

7. look, gaze, _____ (st)are

8. nose, trunk, _____ (sn)out

TAKING READING TESTS: FICTION

Directions: Read this passage about Norma. Then answer questions 1–3.

Wind threw drops of rain against the window. Norma looked up from the book she was reading. She thought she'd heard a tapping at the door. She put down her book and went into the hall. But when she opened the door, no one was there.

Norma was about to close the door when she heard a pitiful mew. Looking down, she saw the neighbor's wet, bedraggled kitten. "Oh, you poor thing!" Norma cried. She picked up the kitten and brought it inside, closing the door behind her. Norma dried the kitten with a soft towel. She was spooning tuna into a dish when her mother entered the kitchen.

"What have we here?" her mother asked.

"She was lost in the storm and all wet, Mom," Norma said. "Can we keep her?"

"She's pretty, isn't she?" answered Mother.

1. Where does this story take place?
   - (a) at Norma's house
   - (b) in a pet store
   - (c) at Norma's mother's office
   - (d) in a street

2. Why did Norma go to the door and open it?
   - (a) She heard the doorbell ring.
   - (b) She heard a kitten mew.
   - (c) She heard a tapping sound.
   - (d) Her mother was coming home.

3. How do Norma and her mother feel about cats?
   - (a) Norma likes cats, but her mother doesn't.
   - (b) Neither of them likes cats.
   - (c) Both of them like cats.
   - (d) Norma's mother likes cats, but Norma doesn't.

MATCH IT UP

Draw a line from each word on the left to its definition on the right.

1. legend

2. pueblo

3. ancestor

4. tribe

5. ancient

6. storyteller

7. remember

a. a group of people with the same ancestors, customs, and language

b. a story that is handed down through the years

c. a Native American village that is made up of stone or adobe buildings built one above the other

d. a person from whom one is descended

e. to bring back to mind

f. very old or from very long ago

g. a person who tells stories for fun or learning

Write the first paragraph of a story that begins "My people tell a legend about . . ." Use three of the words from the left column.

TAKING A BATH

Read the story. Circle all the words with _th_. Then write each word below and underline _th_. Write each word only once.

It is Thursday and Jenna needs to give Bill a bath. Bill is not a big dog but his fur is thick. In the summer he gets a bath once a month. Last month her brother Ben had the job. Now it's Jenna's turn.

Jenna is wearing her bathing suit. Bill is in the tub and covered with suds. Then it happens. There is a big clap of thunder. In a flash, Bill is out of the tub and running toward the house. Jenna is flat on the ground with soap in her mouth. Before she gets up, the dog is through the screen door. Jenna hears her father's shriek as Bill jumps on him.

The story has a happy ending. Dad brings Bill out on the leash and together they rinse him off in the rain.

Thursday	_brother_	_with_
bath	_bathing_	_mouth_
thick	_Then_	_through_
the	_There_	_father's_
month	_thunder_	_together_
		they

POSTER COPY

You're helping to organize an oral history project. You need to make a poster to put up at the senior citizen center asking for volunteers to share their stories. Use the organizer below to plan what to write on your poster.

Who is organizing the project?
Whom should volunteers call?

What is the project about?

Why should people want to participate?

What kind of stories do you want to hear?

 Did I explain what the project is?

Have I included information that will encourage people to participate?

Name

WHAT'S THE STORY?

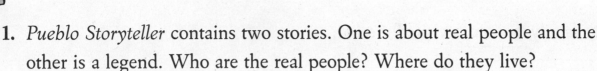

1. *Pueblo Storyteller* contains two stories. One is about real people and the other is a legend. Who are the real people? Where do they live?

   April and her family are members of the Cochiti tribe, a Native American people

   who live in the Cochiti pueblo near Santa Fe, New Mexico.

2. If you didn't know that "How the People Came to Earth" is a legend, what clues in the story would tell you?

   Long Sash is the star called Orion. His people travel on the Milky Way, a band of

   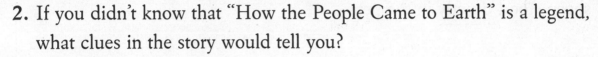
   stars. Spider Woman helps them find their new home.

3. How did Long Sash know that he and his people had found their home?

   He found the markings of the spiderweb on the turtle's back, and tracks that looked

   like those of the mole.

4. What items that are mentioned in *Clues to the Past: A to Z* would you include in this legend if you retold it? Why?

   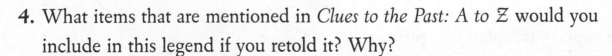
   Possible answers: arrowheads for protection against enemies; basket and olla, for

   keeping house; map for finding their way; quilt for telling their story.

ADVERBS THAT TELL "HOW"

Some adverbs tell how something happened.
Underline these adverbs.

> An adverb is a word that describes a verb. Adverbs can tell how an action happened. Most adverbs that tell *how* end in **-ly.**

1. Our family <u>excitedly</u> visited the fair.

2. We <u>patiently</u> watched for Uncle Joe.

3. He <u>finally</u> arrived with his sheep.

4. His sheep stood <u>quietly</u> in the pen.

5. Uncle Joe <u>quickly</u> prepared his shears.

6. He <u>carefully</u> cut the sheep's wool.

7. Workers <u>immediately</u> stacked the wool.

8. We <u>nervously</u> looked toward the judges.

9. Uncle Joe sheared his sheep <u>perfectly</u>.

10. He <u>happily</u> accepted first prize.

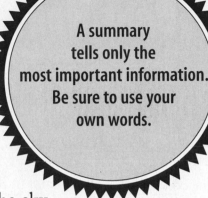

SUMMARIZE IT

Read each paragraph. Write a sentence that tells what the paragraph is about.

Summaries will vary. Sample summaries are given.

A summary tells only the most important information. Be sure to use your own words.

Our earth, sun, and planets are part of the Milky Way galaxy, which has over 100 billion stars. We can see the Milky Way on clear nights if there is no moon and not too many city lights. The Milky Way is a river of stars across the sky that looks like a stream of spilled milk. That's how it got its name.

We are part of a galaxy of 100 billion stars called the Milky Way.

_____

_____

Chuck likes to lie on the grass and look at the stars. He wants to have a telescope. He wants one so much he is saving his money to buy one. It will take a long time, his father said. Chuck knows that. He can wait. He knows the stars will still be there when he finally gets his telescope.

Chuck loves the stars and is saving his money to buy a telescope.

_____

_____

 Write a paragraph about what Chuck thinks about as he looks at the stars.

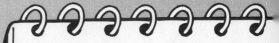

BONE HUNTER

by Alexandra Hanson-Harding
from SCHOLASTIC NEWS

Read the interview below. Use it to complete page 125.

Scholastic News **talked to Dr. Michael Voorhies. He is a paleontologist, or fossil scientist.**

SN: What do paleontologists do?

Michael Voorhies: Bone hunting is what we do. We look for and study fossils. If you're a bone hunter, you keep your eyes on the ground. That's because the things we're interested in are buried in the earth.

SN: What do you do when you find a fossil?

Michael Voorhies: Before we take a fossil out of the ground, we take photographs, make drawings, and study its surroundings. We're interested in the information the fossil can tell us.

SN: Did you want to do this when you were a kid?

Michael Voorhies: Yes, as a matter of fact. I got interested in some of the odd-shaped stones that were in the bottom of the streams. One day I found a petrified tooth and I took it to school. My teacher mailed it to a museum. I got a very nice letter back telling me that this was a giant camel tooth. From then on, this is what I have always wanted to do.

My questions and ideas as I read

Encourage students to use this space to record their questions and ideas as they read.

Copyright © Scholastic Inc.

SUMMARIZE

You are a reporter for your school newspaper. Your job is to write a summary of Michael Voorhies's interview. Use the chart to help you plan your summary. Then write it in the space below.

A summary is a short way of telling about a story in your own words. When you summarize, you tell only the most important ideas.

Name of Article: *Bone Hunter*

Important idea: *Michael Voorhies is a paleontogist.*

Important idea: *Old bones give a lot of information.*

Important idea: *He became interested in bones in school.*

Summary:

Possible answers: Michael Voorhies is a paleontologist, someone who hunts for bones.

He became interested in bones when he was a boy in school. When he finds bones, he studies them and tries to get information from them.

What else do you think Michael Voorhies does in his job? Write your answer in a short summary.

FOLLOW THE CLUES

Use *th* to replace the underlined letters in each word in the box. Write the new word on the line next to its meaning and underline the *th*.

<u>br</u>ing	four<u>teen</u>
fa<u>st</u>er	<u>m</u>ap
pa<u>rk</u>	<u>cr</u>umb
<u>f</u>irst	ear<u>ly</u>
<u>s</u>eem	wea<u>k</u>er

1. _____*earth*_____ The planet on which we live

2. _____*math*_____ The study of numbers

3. _____*them*_____ Those people

4. _____*thing*_____ An object, idea, or event

5. _____*fourth*_____ That which comes between third and fifth

6. _____*father*_____ A male parent

7. _____*weather*_____ For example, "clear and sunny" or "cloudy and raining"

8. _____*path*_____ A trail or track for walking

9. _____*thumb*_____ The short thick finger on each hand

10. _____*thirst*_____ A dry feeling in the mouth caused by a need to drink

CHOOSE REFERENCE SOURCES

If you wanted to learn more about different styles of head coverings from ancient times to now, what kinds of references would you choose?

Circle the sources you might use if you were doing research on hats. Then answer the following questions:

1. Where would you look for information about hats and other clothing?

   How Hats Are Made; Fashion of the Ages; A History of the Hat;

   Encyclopedia vols. F and H; Head Coverings

2. Where would you look for photos of hat factories?

   "How Hats Are Made"

PEASANT WEDDING

Study the picture drawn from a famous painting. Then complete page 129.

LOOK FOR DETAILS IN PICTURES

The picture on page 128 was based on a painting by Pieter Brueghel.
It's called *Peasant Wedding,* and it was painted around 1565.
Study the drawing. Then answer the following questions:

1. How does the title of the painting help you understand the picture?

It explains why the people are eating together.

2. What does the picture tell you about sixteenth-century clothing?

The men are wearing leggings and jackets. The women are wearing dresses

and hats or scarves.

3. What does the picture tell you about sixteenth-century peasant parties?

People are eating together and talking. A man is playing music on a bagpipe. The food

looks simple.

4. What does the picture tell you about sixteenth-century homes?

The furniture is made of rough wood.

The walls appear to be mostly undecorated.

5. What else can you tell about sixteenth-century life, based on the picture?

Students' observations should be supported by the picture. For example, people had

knives; people drank from jugs.

ROY'S TOYS

Read the definition of each word. Then use the words from the box to complete the paragraph.

computer:	an electronic machine that can store information and solve difficult problems quickly
electronic:	having to do with equipment that requires electricity to run, such as radios, televisions, and computers
reprogrammed:	gave new instructions to a computer about how to do its work
solar:	having to do with the sun, the source of heat and light
machines:	equipment we use to do work
robots:	machines that do work formerly done by people

Roy has radios, televisions, and other _____*electronic*_____ equipment at home. He likes to use a _____*computer*_____ to play games, write reports, and do research. Roy's mom _____*reprogrammed*_____ the computer with a new set of instructions. Now Roy wants to search for a CD-ROM that tells how to build _____*robots*_____ that can walk and talk as well as do work. Roy has already built a model car and other _____*machines*_____ that run on _____*solar*_____ power.

Write about using a computer. Use at least two words from the box.

MULTISYLLABIC WORDS

Each syllable, or part of a word, has just one vowel sound. Read each multisyllabic word below. Then answer both questions.

Word	How Many Vowel Sounds?	How Many Syllables?
hurricane	3	3
emergency	4	4
communication	5	5
porcupine	3	3
nevertheless	4	4
magnetize	3	3
unremarkable	5	5
consistent	3	3

E-MAIL MESSAGE: SCHOOLS OF THE FUTURE

Think about what schools will be like 100 years from now. Jot down a few ideas in the box. Then answer the questions.

School Days 100 Years From Now

Electronic Machines	Teachers
_____	_____
_____	_____
_____	_____
_____	_____

School Building	Subject of Study
_____	_____
_____	_____
_____	_____
_____	_____

How might schools of the future be different from schools of today? How might they be the same? _____

_____

_____

What do I expect my reader to learn? Did I include enough information?

Name

OFF IN TIME

1. How does an old book let Margie and Tommy know what school was like long ago?

   It describes what schools were like centuries ago when students met

   in a school building and had real teachers.

2. What major technological change in education does the author think might take place in the future? How do you know?

   Computers will do the work of teachers.

   The author writes about an electronic teacher.

3. How are the illustrations important to this science fiction story?

   The illustrations show what life might be like in the future.

4. For what reasons does Margie think that schoolchildren of the past probably had fun?

   They all went to school together and got to know one

   another and meet new people.

ADVERBS

Adverbs describe verbs. They tell when, where, and how.

A. Look at the examples of adverbs in the box. Then read each adverb below. On the lines write whether it tells *when* or *where*.

Adverbs That Tell Where	Adverbs That Tell When
down, near, there	soon, later, today

1. now _____*when*_____

2. up _____*where*_____

3. sometimes _____*when*_____

4. above _____*where*_____

5. then _____*when*_____

B. Underline the adverbs in the sentences below.

6. The girls left <u>today</u>.

7. The stuffed animal fell <u>down</u>.

8. Robert is <u>here</u>.

9. We used the computer <u>earlier</u>.

10. Tom will arrive <u>late</u>.

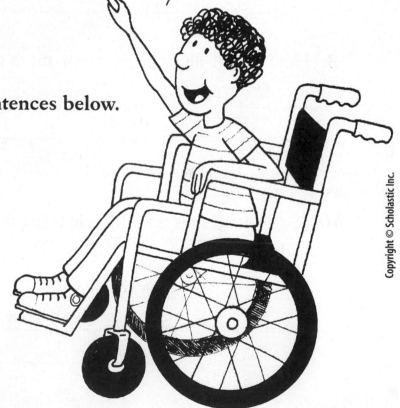

Copyright © Scholastic Inc.

Write a paragraph about an animal that gets into trouble. Use adverbs to describe where and when the animal has its adventures.

SPACE AGE LIFE

Pretend you're living during the Space Age. Write about where you live, what you do, and what you see around you. Draw a picture to go along with what you write.

When you read, look for details that tell you when and where the story takes place.

Students' responses will vary but should include details pertaining to the Space Age.

 How would someone describe your space age home?
Write the description in a paragraph.

STONE AGE SECRETS

by Tonya Leslie from SCHOLASTIC NEWS

Read the article. Use it to complete page 137.

When Jean-Marie Chauvet shone his flashlight on the dark wall of the cave, he was not prepared to see animals in the flickering light. But there on the wall were pictures of 300 beasts! There was a parade of panthers, owls, bears, and other animals. Some animals were painted alone. Other animals were painted together and looked like they were fighting.

Chauvet works with the French government to protect historic caves. He knew right away that this cave was a big discovery.

Why is the cave art so important? It is prehistoric. That means that it was created during a time called the Stone Age.

The cave paintings give clues about prehistoric life. Scientists can tell that people used colorful minerals from the earth to paint the animals different colors. By studying the art, scientists can learn more about the animals that lived back then. Many of them, like woolly rhinos and mammoths, are now extinct.

Chauvet made other discoveries in the cave. He found bones and footprints of ancient cave bears, knives made of stone, and remains of fireplaces. Scientists hope that these discoveries will add pieces to the prehistoric puzzle.

My questions and ideas as I read

Encourage students to use this space to record their questions and ideas as they read.

SETTING

Answer the questions about the setting of
"Stone Age Secrets" on page 136.

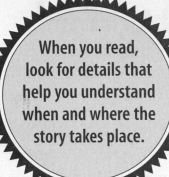

When you read, look for details that help you understand when and where the story takes place.

Where does the story take place? How do you know?

The setting is inside a cave in France. The story says, "on the dark wall of the cave."
It also says, "Chauvet works with the French government to protect historic caves."
So I know it's France.

When does the story take place? How do you know?

It takes place now. I know because Jean-Marie Chauvet has a flashlight,
and flashlights are modern inventions.

What does the place look like?

The cave is dark. Its walls are covered with colorful paintings of animals.
There are also bones and footprints of ancient cave bears, knives made of stone,
and old fireplaces.

Why is this place important to the story?

The story is true. It's about discovering clues to the past in a cave.
So the whole story depends on its setting in a real cave.

Write a short story that begins with the sentence "My flashlight lit up
the dark cave." Describe what you see.

Name

BLAST OFF!

Finish each sentence with a word containing the number of syllables called for. Choose the word and write it on the line.

1. The _____ *astronaut* _____ climbed into the space craft. (3 syllable word)

    investigator   astronaut   classmate

2. The ship _____ *immediately* _____ headed into outer space. (5 syllable word)

    suddenly   quickly   immediately

3. The captain stood on the _____ *observation* _____ deck. (4 syllable word)

    lookout   observation   flight

4. All _____ *passengers* _____ looked out the window. (3 syllable word)

    passengers   people   workers

5. The space trip was an amazing _____ *adventure* _____ . (3 syllable word)

    trip   journey   adventure

6. It led to the _____ *discovery* _____ of another planet. (4 syllable word)

    identification   discovery   selection

BE A BETTER SPEAKER

Use the following questions to help you be a better speaker.

☐ Do I look at my audience? Do I make eye contact and smile?

☐ Do I think about who my audience will be? Do I choose words I think they will understand?

☐ Do I think about the kinds of questions my audience might have and am I prepared to answer them?

☐ Do I know what I'm going to say and how I'm going to say it? Do I either make an outline or write it out word for word?

☐ Do I practice what I'm going to say in front of a mirror?

☐ Do I use body language, gestures, and facial expressions to help my audience understand what I'm saying?

☐ Do I remember to relax and speak slowly and clearly?

WHEN AND WHY DO I NEED TO SPEAK?	HOW CAN I BE A BETTER SPEAKER?	WHAT ADVANTAGE WILL IT GIVE ME?
Students' responses will vary.		

TIME CAPSULE

What are the best artifacts for your time capsule?
What items will give people in the future the
clearest picture of life today? Of course,
the artifacts also should be able to last a long time.
**On the chart below, list all the artifacts you came
up with for your time capsule. Then complete the
chart by answering the questions about each one.**

Item	What does this object tell about life today?	Will this item last a long time?
Students might share their ideas with a partner before filling in the chart.		

HAVE AN OPENING

You've completed your time capsule. Sometime in the future, people will open it. What will they think?

Imagine you are a third grader in the future who is opening the time capsule. Write a description of each object, and tell what you think it was used for.

Answers will vary.

WRITING A MAGAZINE ARTICLE

Think up an event that could happen in the school year 2105. Make up information about it. Use the information to plan a short magazine article. Use the web below to organize your information. Then write your article.

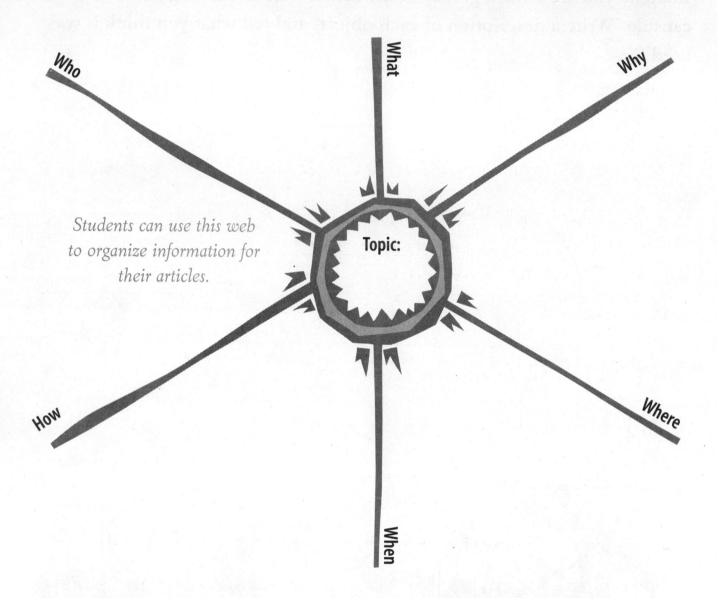

Who

What

Why

Students can use this web to organize information for their articles.

Topic:

How

Where

When

Did I answer the questions *Who, What, When, Where, Why,* and *How*?
Did I present the information in an order that makes sense?

WHAT DID I LEARN?

1. Describe the steps an archaeologist takes to set up a dig.

    Students should indicate an understanding of the basic

    steps, such as choosing a dig site and creating a grid map.

2. What kinds of equipment does an archaeologist need to know how to use?

    Possible answers might include trowels, screening spoons,

    brushes, or measuring tape.

3. What kinds of problems might you face as an archaeologist?

    Students may mention getting permission

    to set up a dig in a certain area or having to work during bad weather.

4. On a separate sheet of paper, draw a picture or write about something you did at the Archaeological Site.

    Answers should refer to a specific activity that the student took part in.

BE A BETTER WRITER

Use the following questions to help you be a better writer.

☐ Do I write about what I know?

☐ Do I try to write every day? Do I keep a journal?

☐ Do I think about why I'm writing each time I write? Do I stick to my purpose?

☐ Do I read? Do I think about stories I like to read, and look at how they're written?

☐ Do I first get my ideas down on paper, and then go back and make my ideas clear? Do I correct the spelling and grammar at the end?

☐ Do I share what I've written with others? Does talking about my writing give me new ideas?

☐ Do I save my writing? Do I go back and reread what I wrote?

WHY DO I NEED TO WRITE?	HOW CAN I BE A BETTER WRITER?	WHAT ADVANTAGE WILL IT GIVE ME?
Answers will vary.		

Copyright © Scholastic Inc.

READER'S LOG

Keep track of books you read about managing information. When you've finished the unit, look over your list. Which book did you like best? Why was it your favorite?

Book Title	Author	Genre	Connection to Managing Information
Answers will vary.			

My favorite book: _____

Reasons why I like this book best: _____

_____

_____

_____

Name

VENN DIAGRAM

Use this organizer to show how two topics or two characters are alike and different.

Answers will vary.

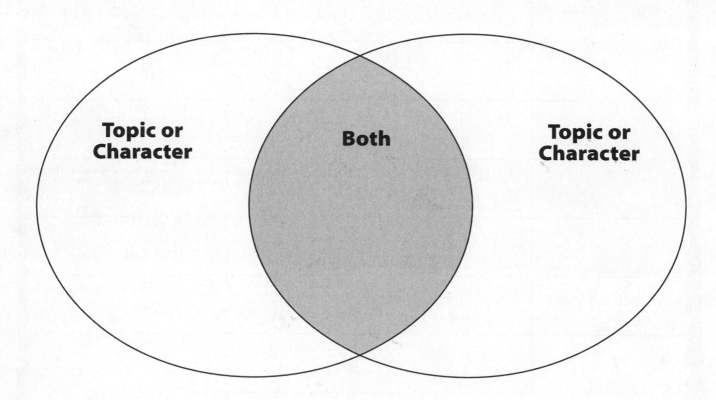

Topic or Character

Both

Topic or Character

★ NEWSLETTER ★

Welcome to *Community Quilt*

Does your street need cleaning? Could your local park use a few more trees? You'll be reading about people who are working to improve their communities. Take a look at what your Anthology has to offer.

A Quiet Hero

There are all kinds of heroes, including some who go about their tasks behind the scenes. In this story, you'll meet one who uses her wisdom to save her village and to win another kind of victory as well.

+PLUS+ **Find out how a young boy keeps his country and his family and friends from certain disaster.**

New Horizons!

You'll discover how immigrants have contributed to communities all over America. You'll also see why Mary McLeod Bethune is a hero to the people of Daytona Beach, Florida.

A famous poet gives a whole new **+PLUS+** meaning to the expression "eating your words." Can words really be as delicious as popcorn?

★ NEWSLETTER ★

Let's Visit a Community Garden

There's a lot more than planting that goes on in a community garden. You'll find out in this Anthology.

Spreading Joy

During the Depression, a young girl far from home plans a secret surprise for her kind, but sad, uncle. Read about how she uses her talent for growing things—and her ability to make the best of a situation—to bring joy to others!

+PLUS+ **Discover what Carnival is like in the Andes and what Carnival is like in St. Paul, Minnesota.**

Meet Lorka Muñoz

The name Lorka means "flower" in Russian. Learn how Lorka Muñoz organizes community gardens in Dayton, Ohio.

Things You'll Do

◆ You'll create an eye-catching **poster** for a community event.

◆ You'll write a **cookbook** of your class's favorite recipes.

◆ You'll make a record of places, people, and events in your community, and design a **community quilt.**

Getting Started

List four things you like about your community. They can be places, people, or celebrations.

1. _____

2. _____

3. _____

4. _____

WELCOME TO THE COMMUNITY GARDEN

1. What do you think you do to plant and care for a garden?

Students may say you have to dig holes and put seeds in the ground. They may

mention watering or weeding as ways to care for a garden.

2. What are some of the tools you think a gardener would use?

Students may mention hoes, shovels, rakes, hoses, or wheelbarrows.

3. What do you want to know about working in a community garden?

Students may want to know what kinds of things they could grow, or who gets

the produce, or who can work in a community garden.

4. Where could you find out more about growing plants for food?

Students may suggest asking a farmer or a gardener. They may also suggest

looking in books.

STUDENT LOG

Here's a way to keep track of what you do in the classroom Community Garden.

Fill in the chart when you visit the Community Garden.

Date	What I Did	What I Learned
_____	_____	_____
_____	_____	_____
_____	_____	_____
_____	_____	_____
_____	_____	_____
_____	_____	_____
_____	_____	_____
_____	_____	_____
_____	_____	_____
_____	_____	_____
_____	_____	_____
_____	_____	_____
_____	_____	_____

WEED WOES!

Write the letter of the definition that matches each word.

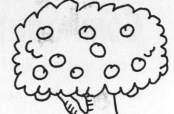

1. orchards ___*c*___   **a.** a straw figure put in a field to frighten away birds

2. plots ___*f*___   **b.** a piece of land having a specific use

3. bouquets ___*e*___   **c.** fields or farms where fruit trees are grown

4. lot ___*b*___   **d.** small books listing things you can buy from a company

5. catalogues ___*d*___   **e.** bunches of picked or cut flowers

6. scarecrow ___*a*___   **f.** small areas of land

 Choose two words from above to use in a sentence about gardening.

COMPOUND CORNFIELD

Read each word below. Each one can be matched with one of the other words on the cornstalk to make a compound word. Write the whole compound word on the lines to the right.

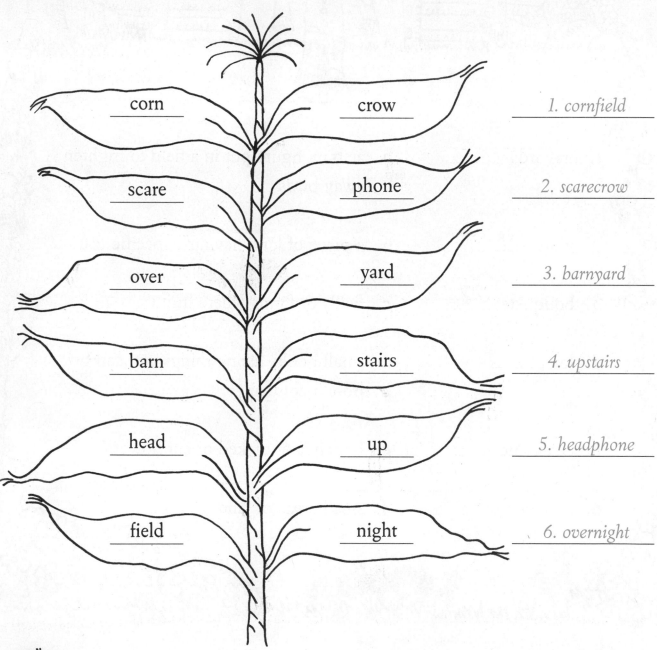

corn

crow

1. cornfield

scare

phone

2. scarecrow

over

yard

3. barnyard

barn

stairs

4. upstairs

head

up

5. headphone

field

night

6. overnight

Make a list of compound words that begin with *back*, such as *backfield*.

CITY LIFE

You have just visited Lydia Grace while she's staying with Uncle Jim. Now you are writing a letter describing where she lives. Include lots of details about the place, and what it looks like.

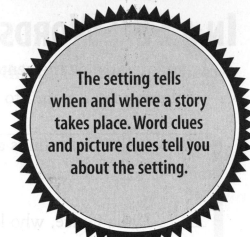

The setting tells when and where a story takes place. Word clues and picture clues tell you about the setting.

Dear_____,

Letters will vary.

_____

_____

_____

_____

_____

_____

_____,

_____

 Write a few sentences telling how Lydia's garden would be different if Uncle Jim had a backyard.

GREAT GARDENS!

You are the community garden director in your town. One of your jobs is to tell people why community gardens are good for a neighborhood. In the space below, design a flyer that tells all the reasons for starting a garden. Decorate your flyer, too.

Flyers will vary.

WILL HE SMILE?

1. What did Lydia want to see on Uncle Jim's face?

   She wanted to see a smile on his face.

2. Name the ways in which Lydia's garden helped the neighborhood and Uncle Jim.

   It made the bakery much prettier, and because of the

   flowers, more people stopped by and bought food from Uncle Jim.

3. Suppose Lydia and Lorka Muñoz worked together to plan a community garden. What do you think it would be like?

   Answers should reflect how both of them want to beautify

   their communities.

4. How do you think Uncle Jim felt about Lydia's leaving? How do you know?

   He was sad to see her go. He baked her a cake and

   hugged her at the train station.

Using *I* and *Me*

Rewrite each sentence using the correct pronoun. Remember to name yourself last.

When you talk about yourself, use the pronoun *I* or *me*. Use *I* in the subject of a sentence. Use *me* in the predicate after the action word. When you also talk about someone else, name yourself last.

1   Ted and (I, me) like to do things together.

Ted and I like to do things together.

2.   Ted's mother looked at Ted and (I, me) cooking pasta.

Ted's mother looked at Ted and me cooking pasta.

3.   My mother shows Ted and (I, me) how to cook rice.

My mother shows Ted and me how to cook rice.

4.   Sometimes my brother and (I, me) help cook dinner.

Sometimes my brother and I help cook dinner.

5.   My brother Ted and (I, me) have a great time cooking.

My brother Ted and I have a great time cooking.

Write a few sentences about yourself and a friend, using the pronouns *I* and *me*.

Name

WHAT HAPPENED?...

Identify the correct inference in each of the following questions. Circle the letter next to the correct answer.

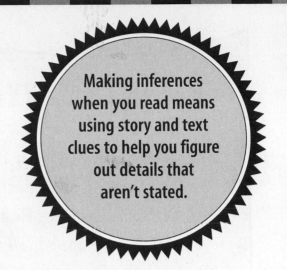
Making inferences when you read means using story and text clues to help you figure out details that aren't stated.

1. Lydia thanks Grandma for the bulbs and says, "You should see them now." **Inference:**

   a. The bulbs arc being baked in the bread.

   b. Otis the cat is sleeping on the bulbs.

   c. The bulbs are beginning to bloom.

2. The people in the neighborhood give Lydia plants and pots. **Inference:**

   a. They want her to sell them.

   b. They want her to plant the flowers in the pots.

   c. They want her to give the plants and pots away.

3. Lydia sweeps the floor in the bakery while Emma washes the windows and Uncle Jim puts pastries on the shelf. **Inference:**

   a. Emma doesn't like to sweep floors.

   b. Lydia doesn't know how to bake.

   c. Everyone helps out with the chores in the bakery.

4. Uncle Jim bakes a cake and brings it up on the roof to Lydia. **Inference:**

   a. Uncle Jim likes to bake.

   b. Uncle Jim is thanking Lydia for the garden.

   c. The cake is for Uncle Jim's birthday.

Copyright © Scholastic Inc.

PICNIC! PARTY! PICK IT UP!

by Greg Kouriakis

Read the poem. Use it to complete page 161.

Here's the story of August fifteenth
In the busiest park in East Summit,
A picnic was planned (all the kids were on hand)
But the park was a mess! Who had done it?
Yes, the park was a mess! Who had done it?

There was trash on the grass, there were peels
    on the paths,
There was plastic wrap, pop cans, and paper.
The people of East Summit all shouted at once,
"Who could have pulled such a caper?"
Yes, who could have pulled such a caper?

So the kids and their parents, and friends from the town,
Gathered coolers and swimsuits and ointment.
Grumbling and fuming, and tearful and hot,
Straggled homeward in great disappointment.
Yes, they straggled homeward in great disappointment.

But the people thought better and returned to the park
And they cleaned up the mess in the grass.
They scraped up the gum and hosed down the paths,
And they even recycled the glass!
Yes, they even recycled the glass!

 My questions and ideas as I read

Encourage students to use this space to record their questions and ideas as they read.

MAKE INFERENCES

Read the narrative poem "Picnic! Party! Pick It Up!" on page 160. Then fill in the chart below.

Use story clues and what you know about a subject to make inferences.

Possible answers:

STORY CLUE	+	WHAT I KNOW	=	INFERENCE
1. Paper, trash, and garbage were scattered around the park.		1. Picnickers usually have pop cans, plastic wrap, and paper.		1. *Earlier picnickers had not cleaned up.*
2. *People were sad, hot, and disappointed.*		2. Nobody can have a good time when the park's a mess.		2. The people were leaving because the park was full of trash.
3. People scraped up gum and recycled glass.		3. *People can work together to solve a problem.*		3. *People felt better about how the park looked after they cleaned it up.*

What inference would you make if the people in the poem had found torn garbage bags at the picnic site?

Name

TWO IN ONE

A. Read each sentence. Circle the compound word. Write the two words that make up each compound word.

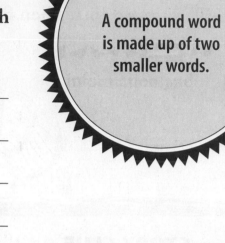

A compound word is made up of two smaller words.

1. I have a new (hairbrush).   _hair_   _brush_

2. He looked in the (shoebox).   _shoe_   _box_

3. Is (anyone) home?   _any_   _one_

4. The (sunshine) feels good.   _sun_   _shine_

5. I broke my (toenail).   _toe_   _nail_

B. Draw a line to connect each word in column 1 to a word in column 2 to make a compound word. Write the new word on the line.

some   call   6. _somebody_

eye   boat   7. _eyesight_

sail   sight   8. _sailboat_

phone   body   9. _phonecall_

play   ground   10. _playground_

CONDUCT AN INTERVIEW

You are preparing to interview a community leader for an article in the school newspaper. Write some questions you will ask during the interview. Use the key words to help you get started.

Person Being Interviewed: _____ *Answers will vary.*

Interview Questions

What _____

_____ ?

When _____

_____ ?

Why _____

_____ ?

Where _____

_____ ?

Who _____

_____ ?

How _____

_____ ?

WRITE A DESCRIPTION

Write a description of a community festival you attended. Include a beginning, a middle, and an end. Answer the questions below to help you plan your description.

Beginning

What kind of festival was it? _____

_____

How did the community prepare for the festival? _____

_____

Middle

What did I see there? _____

_____

What did I hear? smell? taste? _____

_____

What did people do there? _____

_____

End

How did the festival end? _____

_____

Did I tell about a festival I attended?

Did my description have a beginning, a middle, and an end?

Did I use vivid details and action words?

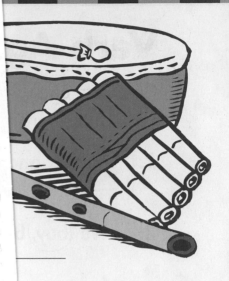

he band to

her with

t Paul Winter

from all over;

nival is an

elling something you like

Verb Agreement

Complete each sentence by circling the correct form of the verb in parentheses ( ).

1. Mother and I (go, goes) shopping.

2. We (buy, buys) new clothes.

3. We (meet, meets) lots of sales people.

4. They (help, helps) us find things.

5. Father (look, looks) for us.

6. We (like, likes) to go to the bookstore.

7. You and I (see, sees) our friend Carrie there.

8. She (wave, waves) to us.

 Write two sentences with subject pronouns t to do with a family member.

Name

WHAT'S YOUR OPINION?

Read the following judgments about *Tonight Is Carnaval*. Then list details from the text and from what you already know to back up each judgment.

When you make a judgment, you form an opinion about the worth or value of something. Base your judgment on something in the text and on what you already know.

JUDGMENT	WHAT FROM THE TEXT SUPPORTS THIS JUDGMENT?	WHAT DO I ALREADY KNOW THAT SUPPORTS THIS JUDGMENT?
Carnaval is lots of fun!	*People wear costumes and will sing and dance for three whole days and nights.*	*I've been to a community celebration before, and it was fun.*
The people of the village are very hard workers.	*They get up each day before it's light and do work; they work hard in the fields; they walk a long way to find wood.*	*Answers will vary.*

You are at Carnaval. Write a letter to a friend telling why you think your friend should or shouldn't come.

HAPPY NEW YEAR

by Meri Wada

Read the story. Use it to complete pages 171 and 173.

Elizabeth was upset. It was New Year's Eve, and her parents had gone to a party without her. Even though she was going to spend the night with Yoko, her best friend, it still wouldn't be the same.

When Elizabeth got to Yoko's house, Yoko was smiling. "Elizabeth," Yoko said. "We're going to have a great New Year—Japanese style."

Elizabeth tried to smile. "If this is a new way to celebrate New Year's Eve, I know I won't like it," she grumbled to herself.

Yoko led Elizabeth into the kitchen. She saw the food that Yoko's family had prepared—broiled fish, rice cakes, pickled vegetables, and many desserts.

Later that night, other friends came to Yoko's house. They ate some of the food. Grandfather taught the girls how to play *karuta,* a Japanese card game. Then the family sang. Yoko's father made everybody laugh by singing off-key.

Suddenly, Elizabeth heard the phone ring. "Elizabeth, it's your mom and dad," said Yoko. Elizabeth couldn't believe it was midnight!

"*Shinen omedeto gozaimasu,*" Elizabeth told her parents. "That's Japanese for 'Happy New Year.' And I want to come back to Yoko's house next year! I had a great time."

My questions and ideas as I read

Encourage students to use this space to record their questions and ideas as they read.

MAKE JUDGMENTS

Read the last paragraph of "Happy New Year" on page 170. Notice what Elizabeth says about celebrating New Year's Eve. Then fill in the chart to help you state your opinion about what Elizabeth meant.

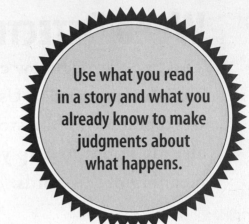

Use what you read in a story and what you already know to make judgments about what happens.

My opinion about what Elizabeth says at the end of "Happy New Year" is:

Possible answer: Elizabeth has learned that celebrating New Year's Eve with friends who do things differently can be fun.

Clues from the text:

Possible answer: Elizabeth takes part in the celebration. She learns to play a new game, sings with the family, and eats the food. She forgets what time it is.

What I already know:

Possible answer: Learning about new customs is fun and interesting. Any celebration with food and singing and games is a great place to be.

If you were Elizabeth, how would you thank Yoko and her family?

Name

WORD DETECTIVE

The two words below come from the story *Tonight Is Carnaval*. Use picture clues and word clues from the story, plus what you already know, to help you figure out the meaning of the words.

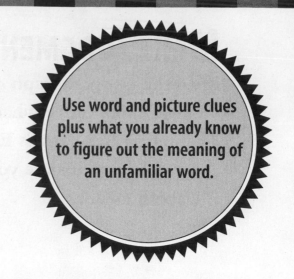

Use word and picture clues plus what you already know to figure out the meaning of an unfamiliar word.

STORY WORD	*charango*	*bombo*
STORY CLUES	*Strings* *"pling pling" sound of kernels hitting bottom of pot* *plays in band*	*"tunk tunk" sound of ax chopping log* *drum* *plays in band*
PICTURE CLUES	*one of the band's instruments is stringed and looks like a guitar*	*one of the band's instruments looks like a large drum played with a big drumstick*
WHAT I ALREADY KNOW	*guitars are stringed musical instruments*	*drums are round musical instruments played by beating with hands or sticks*
MEANING	*small guitar*	*large bass drum*

Draw a picture of one of the words in the story *Tonight Is Carnaval*. See if a partner can guess the meaning of the word.

Context Clues

The sentences below are from "Happy New Year" on page 170. Use word clues in the sentences to find the meaning of the underlined words. Write the meaning of each underlined word. Then tell what clues you used.

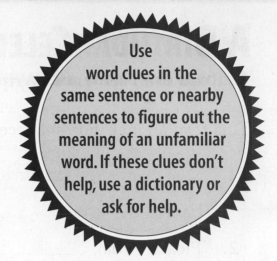

Use word clues in the same sentence or nearby sentences to figure out the meaning of an unfamiliar word. If these clues don't help, use a dictionary or ask for help.

1. Grandfather taught the girls how to play *karuta*, a Japanese card game.

   Meaning: *a Japanese card game*

   Clues: *"play," "a Japanese card game"*

2. Yoko's father made everybody laugh by singing off-key.

   Meaning: *not in the proper tone*

   Clues: *"made everybody laugh," "singing," parts of the compound word*

3. "Shinen omedeto gozaimasu," Elizabeth told her parents. "That's Japanese for 'Happy New Year.'"

   Meaning: *Happy New Year*

   Clues: *"That's Japanese for 'Happy New Year.'"*

Use one of the words or phrases above in a sentence.

Name _____

A BIRTHDAY CELEBRATION

A. Read each sentence. Write a contraction for the words in ( ).

Tina read an invitation she received.

1. "_____*I'm*_____ invited to a birthday party at Jason's house!" she said.
(I am)

2. "Please, Mom, _____*I've*_____ got to go because Jason is a good
friend." (I have)

3. "Sure, _____*that's*_____ fine," said her mother. (that is)

4. "I am sure _____*you'll*_____ have a great time. Who else will be there?"
(you will)

5. "I _____*don't*_____ know," Tina said. (do not)

6. "_____*I'll*_____ call Grant and find out." (I will)

7. "I know _____*they're*_____ best friends." (they are)

**B. Answer each question. Use an apostrophe in your answer to show the
possessive form.**

8. Whose party is it? _____*Jason's party*_____

9. Whose invitation is it? _____*Tina's invitation*_____

10. Where will the party take place? _____*Jason's house*_____

BE A BETTER SPEAKER

Use the following questions to help you be a better speaker.

☐ Do I look at my audience? Do I make eye contact and smile?

☐ Do I think about who my audience will be? Do I choose words I think they will understand?

☐ Do I think about the kinds of questions my audience might have and am I prepared to answer them?

☐ Do I know what I'm going to say and how I'm going to say it? Do I either make an outline or write it out word for word?

☐ Do I practice what I'm going to say in front of a mirror?

☐ Do I use body language, gestures, and facial expressions to help my audience understand what I'm saying?

☐ Do I remember to relax and speak slowly and clearly?

WHEN AND WHY DO I NEED TO SPEAK?	HOW CAN I BE A BETTER SPEAKER?	WHAT ADVANTAGE WILL IT GIVE ME?
Students' responses will vary.		

SCOUT LOCATIONS FOR A VIDEO

Imagine you're making a video about your town. What would you want the audience to see? What people, places, and special events make your town fun and interesting?

Complete the chart. Fill in the people, places, and special events you'd film for your video.

People	Places	Special Events
Answers will vary.		

ADVERTISE YOUR VIDEO

Congratulations! Your video about your community is finished. It's ready to show. Now you need to make posters that advertise it.

The poster should show a symbol of your community. A symbol represents something. When people see the symbol, it should make them think of your community. It should remind them of the good things in your community.

Draw a poster for your video. Be sure to put your community's symbol on it.

Explain how your symbol represents your community.

Students should explain how their choice represents the community.

_____

_____

_____

WORD WISE

Read the clues and fill in the puzzle.

respect   conquer   prospered

warriors   fierce   procession

DOWN

1. frightening and dangerous
2. became successful
5. to defeat and take control of an enemy

ACROSS

3. soldiers, or people who are experienced in fighting battles
4. a feeling of admiration
6. a number of people walking or driving along a street

¹f
i
e
²p   r   c
³w a r r i o r s
o   c
s   e
⁴r e s p e c t   ⁵c
p   o
⁶p r o c e s s i o n
e   q
d   u
e
r

A MISSING CAT

Harry put up a notice about his lost cat. Some of the words are missing.
Write each missing word shown in parentheses. Be sure to add the
correct *-ed* **or** *-ing* **ending. The first one has been done for you.**

TO: Everyone

FROM: Harry

I need your help. Blackie is _____missing_____ ! She _____*disappeared*_____
(miss)   (disappear)

late last night while it was _____*thundering*_____ and _____*raining*_____ . With
(thunder)   (rain)

each flash of lightning the cat _____*meowed*_____ . The last time I saw her she
(meow)

was _____*running*_____ under my bed. I _____*planned*_____ to go to bed early,
(run)   (plan)

but I spent the whole night _____*looking*_____ for Blackie. If you find my cat
(look)

for me, you will be _____*rewarded*_____ as a hero!
(reward)

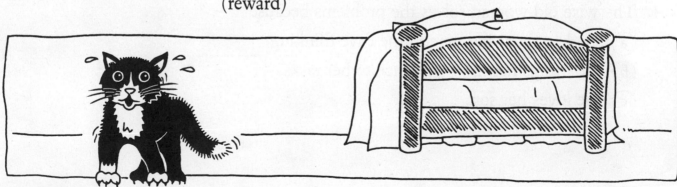

Write a paragraph about finding the cat. Use lots of words that end
with *-ed,* and *-ing.*

HOW DO YOU KNOW?

Make inferences as you answer the following questions. Fill in the letter that correctly completes each statement.

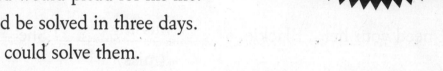

Making inferences when you read a story means using story clues and what you already know to figure things out on your own.

1. When Lord Higa gave out the three impossible tasks, he thought that
   (a) the cruel young lord would plead for his life.
   (b) the problems would be solved in three days.
   (c) few, if any, people could solve them.

2. After the cruel young lord asked six wise men to solve the problems, he thought
   (a) the men wouldn't be able to solve the problems in time.
   (b) the men would ask others for help.
   (c) the men could perform the impossible tasks.

3. When the young farmer told the cruel young lord that he hid his mother, the farmer thought that
   (a) the cruel young lord would reward him.
   (b) the cruel young lord would punish him.
   (c) Lord Higa would ride into town.

4. The wise old woman solves the problems because
   (a) she has spent her time in the cave thinking.
   (b) she brings her life experience to her tasks.
   (c) she loves her son.

Explain in your own words why elderly people are very valuable community members.

A HEROIC DEED

Create your own heroic deed for a story. Begin by naming a hero.
Imagine the problem that he or she will face. Tell how the hero saves the
day by solving the major problem in the story.

Hero:
_____

Problem:
_____
_____
_____

Heroic Deed:
_____
_____
_____

Solution:
_____
_____
_____

Is the heroic deed true to life or something that can't really happen?

THE HOLE STORY

Answer each question below to explain the plot of "The Little Hero of Holland."

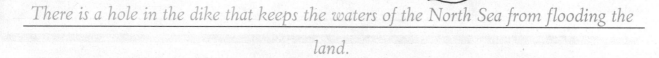

1. Who is the main character?

   The main character is a young boy named Peter.

2. What is the setting?

   The setting is Holland, a long time ago.

3. What is the problem?

   There is a hole in the dike that keeps the waters of the North Sea from flooding the land.

4. How does the character act to solve the problem?

   He sticks his finger in the dike and keeps it there until help arrives.

5. How is the problem finally solved?

   A passerby sees the problem and calls on others to come fix the dike.

6. What happens at the end of the story?

   The townspeople cheer their little hero.

STAR OF THE DAY

1. How does the wise old woman become the community hero?

   She performs the three impossible tasks that the cruel Lord Higa sets forth.

   She therefore prevents him from conquering the village.

2. In what way is the young farmer also a hero?

   He saves his mother from death when the cruel lord orders that everyone over the

   age of seventy be taken into the mountains to die. He hides her in a cave that

   he digs under the kitchen.

3. How does the folk tale prove the old saying that "Wisdom comes with age"?

   Her long lifetime of knowledge helped the old woman solve each task.

4. What lesson does the folk tale teach about people in the community?

   We should value all people, including the elderly.

Adjectives: Comparisons

> To compare two things, add **-er** to the adjective or use the word **more**. To compare three or more things, add **-est** to the adjective or use the word **most**.

A. Complete the chart below. Write the missing adjectives on the lines.

	Adjective	Compares Two	Compares Three or More
1.	deep	*deeper*	**deepest**
2.	great	*greater*	*greatest*
3.	beautiful	**more beautiful**	*most beautiful*
4.	fast	*faster*	*fastest*
5.	active	*more active*	*most active*

B. Circle the correct form of the adjective in parentheses ( ).

6. Knute Rockne was one of the (greater/**greatest**) football coaches ever.

7. The inventor of the telephone was (**quicker**/quickest) than others to see that it was needed.

8. Irving Berlin wrote some of the world's (greater/**greatest**) songs.

9. The volcano in Hawaii was (**more active**/most active) than the one in the state of Washington.

10. She is the (smarter/**smartest**) woman in the world.

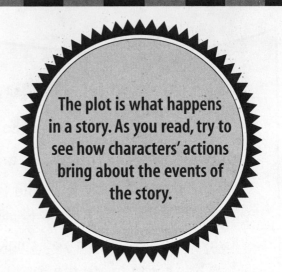
IMAGINE THAT!

Suppose that the little boy did not try to stop the leak in the dike. What if he ran for help instead? How could his actions change the plot of the story? In the space below, make some notes about the new plot.

The plot is what happens in a story. As you read, try to see how characters' actions bring about the events of the story.

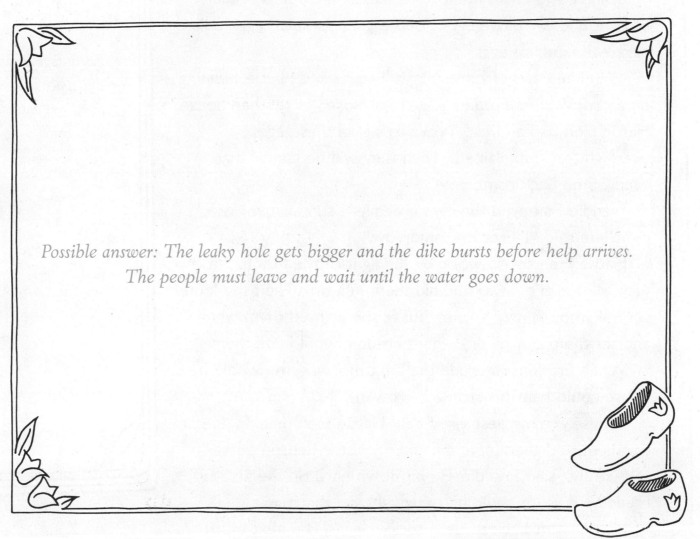

Possible answer: The leaky hole gets bigger and the dike bursts before help arrives. The people must leave and wait until the water goes down.

What other problems in this land of canals and dikes might the little boy have faced? Describe them.

ACTIVE READING

Read the story. Use it to complete page 187.

Freddie Fox and Hattie Hen

Early one morning Freddie Fox snuck up to the hen house. As he tiptoed quietly along, Hattie Hen spotted his bushy tail. "Where do you think you're going?" she cried out.

"Didn't you invite me for breakfast?" answered Freddie Fox. "You know I love eggs. Fried eggs, scrambled eggs, boiled eggs—all kinds of eggs."

"You keep away from my eggs!" squawked Hattie, jumping up and down. As Freddie Fox crept closer to the hen house, Hattie Hen had an idea. "I have to sit on these eggs overnight," she explained. "Then they will be tastier than ever. Come back tomorrow."

Freddie Fox eyed the eggs greedily. "I suppose you're right," he said. "I'll return tomorrow."

Hattie Hen set to work. By the light of the moon, she took all her eggs away and hid them in a box. Then she found several smooth, oval stones. Busily, she painted them white and set them out to dry where Freddie would find them.

When Freddie returned the next morning, the whole hen house could hear his stomach growling.

"These are my best eggs," said Hattie Hen meekly. "Please eat them, and then leave me and my sister hens in peace."

"Gladly," said Freddie. He bit down hard on the first egg. Freddie's scream could be heard all over the farm.

Hattie went back to her precious eggs. The next morning, four chicks were born!

My questions and ideas as I read

Encourage students to use this space to record their questions and ideas as they read.

Copyright © Scholastic Inc.

PLOT

Fill in the plot chart for "Freddie Fox and
Hattie Hen" on page 186.

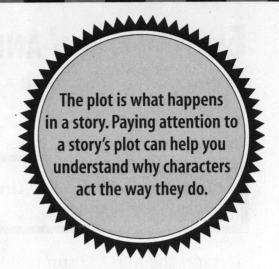

The plot is what happens
in a story. Paying attention to
a story's plot can help you
understand why characters
act the way they do.

Characters: *Freddie Fox and Hattie Hen*	
Setting: *hen house on a farm*	
Problem: *Freddie wants to eat Hattie's eggs.*	
Plot Events: *1. Hattie tells Freddie she needs to sit on eggs overnight.* *2. Hattie sets out stones and paints them to look like eggs.*	
How Problem Is Solved: *Freddie bites down on stone and screams in pain.* *Hattie's eggs are saved.*	

"Freddie Fox and Hattie Hen" is a fable, a short story that teaches a
lesson. Write the lesson that Freddie Fox has learned.

Name

ENDINGS: -ed AND -ing

Complete each verse with a word that rhymes. Add -ed or -ing to the base words below.

plan wait spill thunder wink

1. Over the hills the sun is sinking.
   Up in the sky the stars are _____*winking*_____.

2. The scouts made sure their hooks were baited.
   Then they cast out their lines and
   _____*waited*_____.

3. Cleaning up the den was just grand.
   But cleaning the attic was not what we
   _____*planned*_____.

4. "Will the storm end soon?" I am wondering.
   The lightning is flashing, and the noise is
   _____*thundering*_____.

5. First make sure the pitcher is filled.
   Then hold it tight so no water is _____*spilled*_____.

TEST-TAKING: LANGUAGE ARTS

Carefully read each set of directions. Then mark your answer choice.

Capitalization

Directions: Read the sentences and look at the underlined words. If the underlined words are correct, fill in the circle for D, "Correct as is." If there is a mistake in capitalization, fill in the circle for the letter choice that shows correct capitalization.

---

1 Eric went to see dr. Adams.

(a) Dr. adams
(b) Dr. Adams
(c) dr. adams
(d) Correct as is.

2 The office was closed on Thanksgiving Day.

(a) Thanksgiving day
(b) thanksgiving day
(c) thanksgiving Day
(d) Correct as is.

Spelling

Directions: Read each sentence. Look to see if each underlined word is spelled correctly. Fill in the bubble beneath any misspelled word. If all the words are spelled correctly, fill in Answer D, "No mistake."

1 Did you hear somethin strange? No mistake.

     (a)   **(b)**   (c)   (d)

2 The children didn't beleave the story. No mistake.

   (a)   **(b)**   (c)   (d)

NEW WORDS

Pick a word from the box that fits each clue.

foreign: from another country

inspectors: people who look over official papers with care

advertisements: public announcements that describe a product or service for sale

migrate: to move from one country to another

newcomers: people who have recently arrived in a place

1. Someone might get a job or buy a new coat after reading one of these.

   advertisements

2. This is another name to describe new neighbors.

   newcomers

3. This word describes what people who move from another country to the United States do. _migrate_

4. If you were going to another country, these people would examine your passport at the border. _inspectors_

5. This word describes languages from another country.

   foreign

 Use three words from the box to write about a family that moves from another country to your town.

Name

BREAK IT UP!

Read the words on the tree trunk. Draw a line showing where the word is divided.

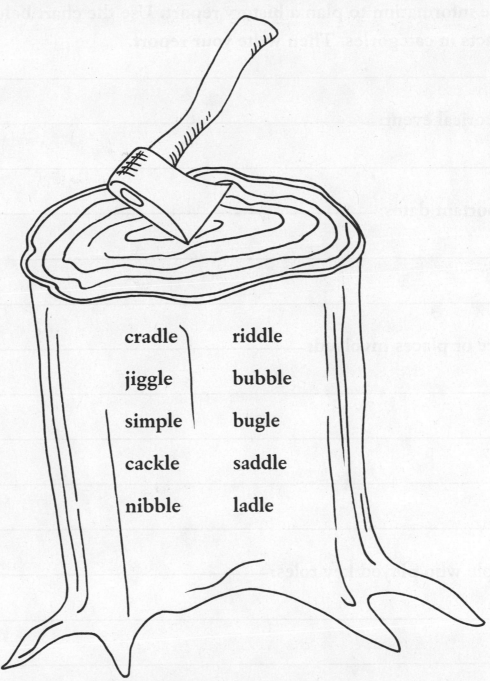

cradle   riddle

jiggle   bubble

simple   bugle

cackle   saddle

nibble   ladle

cra/dle; sim/ple; nib/ble bub/ble; sad/dle;
cack/le; jig/gle; rid/dle; bu/gle; la/dle

WRITE A HISTORY REPORT

Choose a historical event that interests you, and find information about it. Use the information to plan a history report. Use the chart below to put your facts in categories. Then write your report.

Historical event: _____

_____

Important dates: _____

_____

_____

Place or places involved: _____

_____

_____

_____

_____

People who played key roles: _____

_____

_____

_____

_____

STRANGERS IN A NEW LAND

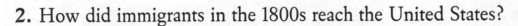

1. Why did so many people want to come to the United States to live?

   Many came to find work; wages were high in the

   United States; land was cheap and plentiful.

2. How did immigrants in the 1800s reach the United States?

   They came on sailing ships until the mid-1800s, and later they came on steamships.

3. What did immigrants bring to the United States?

   They brought bedding, clothes, and food, in baskets, boxes, and sacks.

   Some brought special favorites, such as books or toys.

4. In what ways was Ellis Island like a small city?

   It had dormitories, restaurants, a hospital, a post office, banks, laundries, and so on.

5. In what ways did immigrants contribute to the American way of life?

   They brought new words to the language; they introduced log cabins,

   ice skating, orchestras, and so on.

Irregular Verbs with Have, Has, or Had

On each line below, write the correct past form of the verb in parentheses ( ). Then circle the helping verb.

> Irregular verbs change their form when they describe an action in the past. Some irregular verbs change form again when used with the helping verbs **have**, **has**, or **had**.

1. Jana (has) ———— *seen* ———— a kite festival. (see)

2. She (has) ———— *gone* ———— with her father to Spring Kites Galore. (go)

3. A man (had) ———— *sold* ———— snacks from a cart. (sell)

4. They (had) ———— *eaten* ———— popcorn as they watched the kites. (eat)

5. The judges (had) ———— *given* ———— three prizes. (give)

6. One prize (had) ———— *gone* ———— to the prettiest kite. (go)

7. Kim (had) ———— *brought* ———— a Chinese box kite. (bring)

8. She (had) ———— *written* ———— her name on all four sides. (write)

9. All the kite fliers (had) ———— *done* ———— their best. (do)

10. Afterwards, everyone (had) ———— *sung* ———— songs. (sing)

ISLAND IDEAS

Reread page 349. In the island, write the main idea of this section. Then write the supporting details in the surrounding boats

They went to the Registry Room.

Doctors and inspectors examined them.

Immigrants were kept busy when they landed at Ellis Island.

They exchanged foreign money.

They bathed and did their laundry.

FIORELLO LA GUARDIA

by Sal Calciano

Read the story. Use it to complete page 197.

Fiorello La Guardia lived from 1882 to 1947. He was born in New York, but spent part of his early life in Europe. He moved back to New York to study law.

When he finished law school, La Guardia set up a law office. Later, he became a member of Congress and then mayor of New York City.

While La Guardia was a political leader, he worked very hard to make New York City a better place to live in. New playgrounds were built. He created jobs for many people who were out of work. Some people planted trees and shrubs in city parks. Others built new bridges, tunnels, highways, and houses.

Fiorello La Guardia is one of New York City's best-remembered mayors. Today there is an airport in New York, La Guardia Airport, named after him.

My questions and ideas as I read

Encourage students to use this space to record their questions and ideas as they read.

Name

MAIN IDEA/DETAILS

Write the main idea of the story "Fiorello La Guardia" in the center circle. Write the details that support the main idea in the surrounding circles.

The main idea is the most important idea of a paragraph, section, or story.

Detail
He became a member of Congress and then a mayor.

Detail
He worked very hard to make New York City a better place to live in.

Main Idea
La Guardia was one of New York City's best-remembered mayors.

Detail
He had many new playgrounds built in New York.

Detail
He created work for many jobless people.

Detail
An airport was named after him.

How do you think the people of New York City felt about Mayor La Guardia? Why?

Name

SNIP THE SYLLABLES!

Divide the words into syllables by drawing a line where the scissors should cut

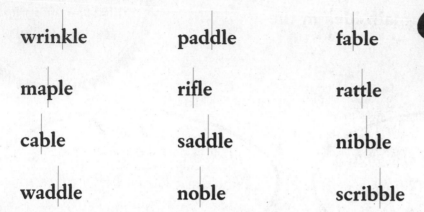

wrin|kle   pad|dle   fa|ble

ma|ple   ri|fle   rat|tle

ca|ble   sad|dle   nib|ble

wad|dle   no|ble   scrib|ble

Now think of four or five words that end with a consonant + *le*. Show where the word should be divided by drawing a line between the syllables.

Possible answer: pud/dle, bub/ble, la/dle
_____

jig/gle, cra/dle
_____

_____

_____

Name

USE ENCYCLOPEDIAS

Read the encyclopedia article. Then answer the questions below.

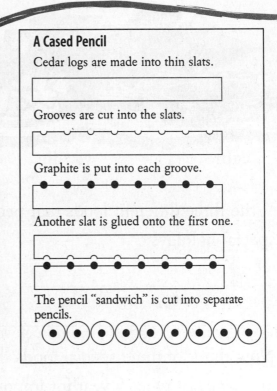

214 Pencil

Pencil A pencil is the most widely used writing and drawing instrument in the world. People use pencils to write words, numbers, and pictures. Each year ten billion pencils are produced in the world.

Making a Pencil Cased pencils are made of a black writing substance surrounded by wood. The black substance is graphite mixed with clay. Graphite for pencils is formed into spaghetti-like strings, cut to the right length, and dried. The wooden casing for pencils is made of cedar because it sharpens easily.

History The earliest pencils were used by the Greeks and Romans. They used flat cakes of lead to make marks. Graphite was discovered in the 1500s. The first pencil made of a wooden case glued around a line of graphite was made in the late 1700s. In 1861, Eberhard Faber built the first pencil factory in the United States.

See also Eraser; Faber; Graphite

A Cased Pencil

Cedar logs are made into thin slats.

Grooves are cut into the slats.

Graphite is put into each groove.

Another slat is glued onto the first one.

The pencil "sandwich" is cut into separate pencils.

1. What do the headings tell you?

The headings tell you what information is found in the paragraphs beneath them.

2. What does the diagram tell you about a pencil?

The diagram tells you how a pencil is made.

3. Where could you look if you did not find the information you wanted in this article?

You could look for other articles mentioned in the "See also" reference.

PICK FOODS FOR A CLASS BANQUET

Plan a holiday banquet with your class! What kinds of foods will you include?

Answers will vary.

1. Write three different foods that people serve when they get together for special holidays.

_____

_____

2. Now think of three special foods that are prepared at your house, maybe only once or twice a year for important occasions.

_____

_____

3. Name some foods or snacks that you know how to prepare.

_____

_____

4. Now, with all that food on your mind, pick three foods that you'd most like to include in a class banquet.

_____

_____

PLAN A CLASS BANQUET

On page 200, you chose the food for your class banquet. What will you serve so that everyone in the class gets to eat at least one favorite food?

Complete the following steps:

1. Fill in the foods you picked. Decide whether they should be served at the beginning, middle, or end of the meal, or just as an extra treat.

2. Next, go to other students in your class and find out what their food choices were. Write them on the chart in the category they fit best.

3. After you've filled in all the spaces, put a line through any foods that appear more than once on the chart.

4. Now select three items from each category for your final menu. Enjoy the banquet!

BANQUET MENU POSSIBILITIES

Before the Main Course	With the Main Course	After the Main Course	Extra
Answers will vary.			

LEARN AND HAVE FUN!

Fill in each blank with a word from the box.

elementary: in school, having to do with kindergarten through grades four, five, or six

programs: shows seen in theaters or on television or heard on the radio

recited: spoken from memory in front of people

audiences: groups of people gathered in a place to hear or see something

campus: the grounds and buildings of a school, such as a college

teachers: people who teach in a school or college

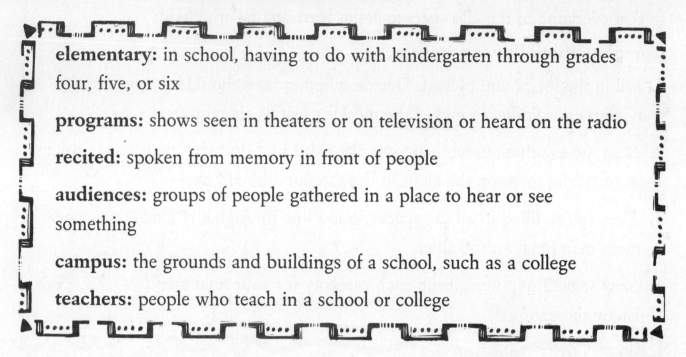

These people give you homework:

teachers

Words that have to do with an auditorium:

audiences

recited

programs

The school is part of this:

campus

Having to do with the grades in your school:

elementary

Use at least three words from the box to write about an event that takes place in a school auditorium.

3-LETTER BLENDS

A. In each box, replace the underlined letter or letters with the 3-letter blend given. Then write the word on the line.

spr	str	squ
<u>m</u>ay: _spray_	<u>l</u>ike: _strike_	<u>p</u>eak: _squeak_
<u>p</u>ain: _sprain_	<u>th</u>ing: _string_	<u>f</u>are: _square_
<u>s</u>ang: _sprang_	<u>f</u>etch: _stretch_	s<u>n</u>eeze: _squeeze_
<u>w</u>rinkle: _sprinkle_	<u>b</u>eam: _stream_	<u>p</u>int: _squint_

B. Use some of the words you wrote above to answer each phrase.

1. not a circle, but a _____ _square_ _____

2. not a big river, but a small _____ _stream_ _____

3. not a loud screech, but a soft _____ _squeak_ _____

4. not a ball of yarn, but a piece of _____ _string_ _____

5. not a hit, but a _____ _strike_ _____

Choose five other words from the box. Write their definitions.

FILL IN THE DETAILS

Below are two main ideas from *Mary McLeod Bethune*. Write story details that support each of these ideas.

The main idea is the most important point the author is trying to make. Details support the main idea.

MAIN IDEA:

In 1904 Mrs. Bethune opened her school, called Daytona Normal and Industrial School for Girls.

Supporting Details:

*Possible answers:
Mrs. Bethune rang a bell to show it was time for school to start; five girls came to the school; the teacher and students used wooden boxes for desks and chairs; the children loved the school.*

MAIN IDEA:

Mrs. Bethune tried hard to raise money for her school.

Supporting Details:

Possible answers: The students made ice cream and pies to sell; they gave programs at hotels and in churches; Mrs. Bethune bought a used bicycle and rode all over Daytona Beach, knocking on doors and asking people for their help.

Think of another biography you have read. What were some of the main ideas? What were some of the supporting details?

BIOGRAPHY

Write a biography of a family member, a friend, or a classmate. Ask the person the following questions to help you get started. Add two more questions that you would like the person to answer. Use the questions to help you write the biography.

1. What was the most important event in your life?

2. Is there a person who has made your life better or easier? Who is it? What did the person do for you?

3. What facts do you think people would like to know about you?

4. _____ *Students might raise questions about the person's work or* _____

5. _____ *leisure activities.* _____

Do my questions clearly tell the facts about the person?

Do my questions help me to get information for the biography?

Do my questions ask about the most important events in the person's life?

THE GIFT OF A GOOD EXAMPLE

1. Why did Mary McLeod Bethune want to start a school of her own?

She wanted to give young black children a chance

to attend school and learn.

2. What problems did Mary McLeod Bethune have to overcome before she could open her first school?

She had no money, and the only building she could find needed many repairs.

3. How did the children help Mrs. Bethune open the school and keep it going?

They helped clean the school, and they helped raise money for the

rent and for school supplies.

4. Why did Mrs. Bethune decide to open a hospital?

She opened a hospital for African Americans after one of her students

became ill and was not allowed to stay in a white hospital.

Name _____

Expanding Sentences

Combine each pair of short sentences to
make one longer sentence. Write it on the line.

> When two sentences have the same subject, the sentences can be combined by joining their subjects with the word **and**. When two sentences have the same verb, the sentences can be combined by joining the verbs with the words **and** or **but**.

1. Sammy works in the garden. Lisa works in the garden.

Sammy and Lisa work in the garden.

2. Sammy planted seeds. Sammy watered them daily.

Sammy planted seeds and watered them daily.

3. The carrots are ripe now. The tomatoes can't be eaten yet.

The carrots are ripe now, but the tomatoes can't be eaten yet.

4. Lisa hung a birdhouse from the tree. Lisa put bird seed inside.

Lisa hung a birdhouse from the tree and put bird seed inside.

5. The birds visit the birdhouse. The birds sing beautiful songs.

The birds visit the birdhouse and sing beautiful songs.

6. I worked hard in the garden. It looks pretty.

I worked hard in the garden, and it looks pretty.

Write two short sentences about flowers. Then combine the sentences
into one expanded sentence.

HERE'S WHAT I WANT YOU TO KNOW. . . .

Eloise Greenfield, author of *Mary McLeod Bethune,* is going to give a speech and slide show at your school. What do you think she should talk to the students about? What types of slides should she show? Write your ideas below.

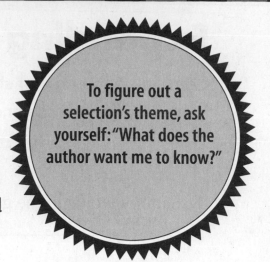

To figure out a selection's theme, ask yourself: "What does the author want me to know?"

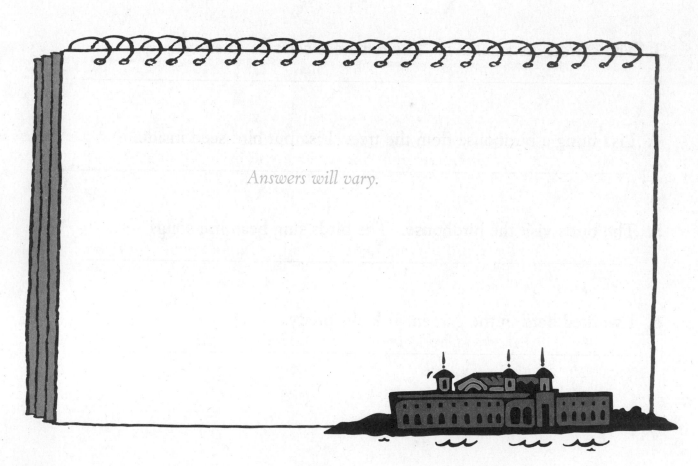

Answers will vary.

Write a short letter to a friend describing the slide show Eloise Greenfield gave to your school.

COMING TO AMERICA

from *Scholastic News*
Read the article. Use it to complete page 210.

Joseph Verbo arrived in America in August 1947, when he was twelve years old. *Scholastic News* talked to Joseph about his journey and his memories of Ellis Island.

Joseph and his family came on an American naval ship from Sicily, Italy. After 15 days on board, they arrived in America. Joseph remembers standing on a crowded deck with his two brothers. "We were holding on tightly to my mother. People were cheering and pointing towards the Statue of Liberty."

Joseph and his family were taken by ferryboat to Ellis Island. "We were interviewed by immigration officials and examined by doctors." Joseph's mother told him that they had to wait for their uncle who was already in America to come and get them.

Joseph and his family waited in the detention center on Ellis Island. It was crowded and noisy. They waited there for 13 days. Finally, one evening, his uncle came to get them. "As we looked at the city lights just across the harbor, I remember thinking that at last we were home!"

My questions and ideas as I read

Encourage students to use this space to record their questions and ideas as they read.

Copyright © Scholastic Inc.

THEME

Read the questions below. Think about the author's message in the article "Coming to America" on page 209. Then write your answers in each box.

> The theme is the message about life or nature that the author wants you to get from the story.

How did Joseph Verbo come to America?

He left his country, Italy. He took a long journey on a ship.

What happened to Joseph and his family after they arrived at Ellis Island?

Officials asked them questions. Doctors examined them.

How did Joseph feel when his uncle arrived?

He was happy to be in America. He felt that he finally had a home.

What message is the author giving me?

Finding a new home in America was worth the wait at Ellis Island.

Do you think it was worth the long trip to come to America? Explain your answer.

Name

THREE-LETTER BLENDS

Read the words below. Then fill the school bus with all the words that contain three-letter blends.

sprain	strike	spray	street
rain	slim	play	squint
strain	squish	plate	stop
stain	quick	straight	pint

sprain strike spray street

squint strain squish straight

SCHOOL

GENERATE QUESTIONS FOR RESEARCH

Think of a main question you'd like to research. Complete the organizer below by asking other detailed questions. Then decide which resources would best help you answer these questions.

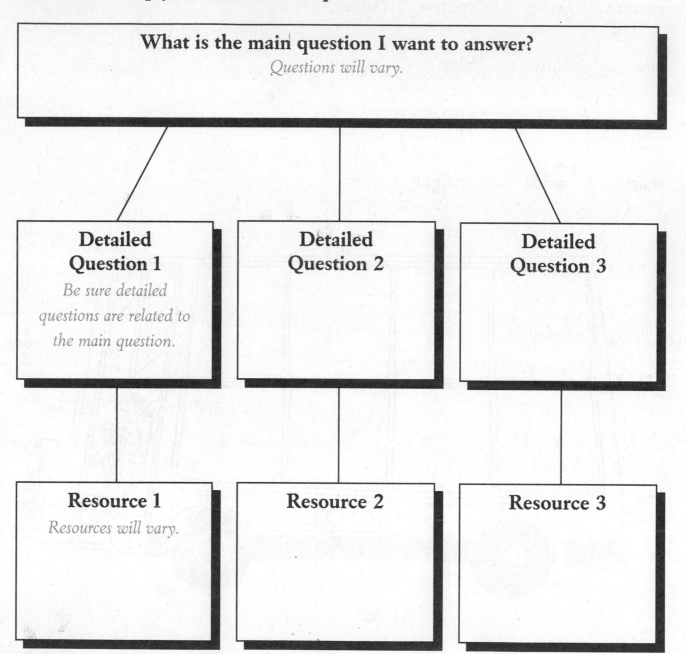

What is the main question I want to answer?
Questions will vary.

Detailed Question 1
Be sure detailed questions are related to the main question.

Detailed Question 2

Detailed Question 3

Resource 1
Resources will vary.

Resource 2

Resource 3

Find one of the resources you included in the organizer. Use it to answer a question you asked.

RESEARCH FOR YOUR QUILT SQUARE

It's time to design your quilt square. The first step is to research the topic.

1. What person, place, or activity will you research for your quilt square?

Students should choose a landmark, place, group, person, or activity that represents the community.

2. Where will you go, and whom will you ask, for information on your topic?

Students may find information by visiting the school or local library, or by

interviewing people who have lived in the community a long time.

3. What do you want to find out about your topic? List three questions.

Possible answers: What is it? How long has it been in the community?

What does it do, or how are people involved in it? Why is it important?

How does it relate to the community?

4. Take notes on the information you find. Here are some index cards you can use.

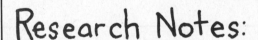

Research Notes:

Research Notes:

SKETCH YOUR QUILT SUBJECT

You've worked hard to find out about a topic for your quilt square.

Now here's a chance to use your research!

Close your eyes for a moment. Imagine different ways to show your quilt topic.

Do you want to put words or other objects around the main picture?

Sketch some of your ideas here.

A

Responses will vary.

B

C

D

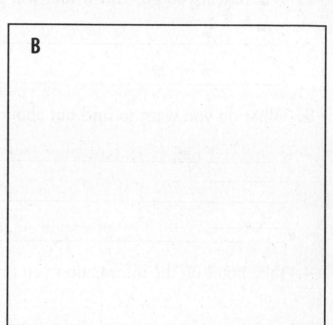

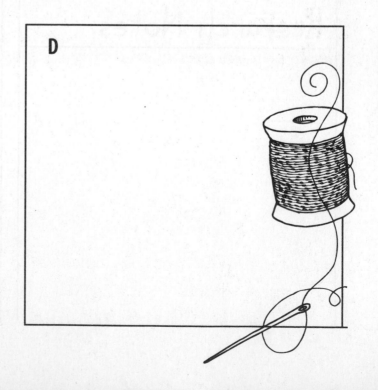

WRITING A POEM

Write a poem about a person who is helpful to your community. Use the charts below to plan your poem.

Whom will I describe?	What does this person do to help others?

How will my poem let readers know what this person is like?

Poetic Description	Example
vivid verbs	
precise adjectives	
repeated words and/or rhymes	
onomatopoeia	

- What details of sight, smell, sound, taste, and touch will I include?
- Should I add more descriptive details?
- Will my poem sound good when read aloud?

BOOK REPORT

Fill in the story-chart book report and add pictures.

Picture **1**   *Answers will vary.*   Picture **2**

Book Title: _____

Author: _____

Illustrator: _____

Tell about the story: _____

_____

_____

_____

_____

_____

_____

_____

_____

_____

Picture **3**   Picture **4**